Daddy duJour

Barbara Hammond

Copyright © 2019 by Barbara Hammond
All rights reserved. No part of this book may be used or reproduced in any manner whatsoever without written permission, except in the case of brief quotations embodied in critical articles or reviews.

Cover: Design by Shoi, Shoi-Yean Mak

Published 2019 by Shorehouse Books
Printed in the United States of America

ISBN-10: 0-9600085-1-9
ISBN-13: 978-0-9600085-1-3

Acknowledgments

This book has been stressful and cathartic at the same time. I've started it many times over the past twenty years or so and, finally it is finished and published. A heartfelt Thank You to Donna Cavanaugh and her team at Shorehouse Books for taking it on and making it happen.

I'm thankful for my husband, Dave who lovingly encouraged me over the years to trust my gut and speak my truth.

I know I couldn't have gotten through my childhood without my grandparents, Mamaw and Granddaddy, and my Uncle Ralph and Aunt Jean. They were always there for me, whenever they knew where we were. And I'll never forget all that I learned at the age of five, thanks to Minnie and Delmar Cox. My six months living with them has stuck with me, in such a good way, ever since.

I want to thank my friend, Suzanne Borrell, who encouraged me to write and helped me with the first draft. Also, Lee Romano Sequeira, for helping me get it started. And, so many other supporters of this project over the years. Thank you, Sonia Marsh, Stephanie Brennan, Annabel Candy, and all who have supported my blog, Zero to 60 and beyond, and pushed for more stories about my childhood.

A huge thank you to Shoi-Yean Mak for her cover art. I'm glad we were on the same wavelength, Shoi!

And, last but not least, I have to thank the man who gave me the name of the book while doing a comedy routine at a friends party. He had asked for some info from the hostess about guests he might be able to mention that had a good sense of humor. I was quite surprised when he called my name during his routine but, it has stuck with me ever since. He asked, "Where is Barbara Hammond?" I reluctantly raised my hand, and he said, "I understand when you write your memoir it's going to be named, Daddy du jour. Your mama got around!" Thank you, whoever you are! My sense of humor has helped me tremendously over the years, believe me!

Chapter

I

Running Away

"I'll take care of putting your things in the trunk, Miss, you take the baby and get in the cab where it's warm," the Taxi driver said.

Warmth.

Something I had longed for through all the horrible winter months. And, here we were making our escape on the coldest night in the history of Toledo, Ohio. It was twenty-three degrees below zero on January twenty-third, nineteen sixty-three. I was twelve, and I could never forget the date.

The taxi had an odd exotic aroma I wasn't familiar with but, it was warm. There were so few times we had been warm this brutal winter. It was heavenly.

I slowly loosened the quilt from my brother, David, and removed his stocking cap. He didn't wake, so I laid him on the seat next to me with his head on my lap. He was so small for a three-year-old, but given our lifestyle, it wasn't a surprise. It would be a fairly long ride, and it was best he slept.

The driver got in, and we were off to, what I hoped would be, a safe haven. My step-father, Al, was trying to take custody of us and, his sister and her husband were going to take care of us during the process. David was Al's son.

Al was mom's third husband. Here we were returning to the town we'd left four months before when mom's affair with a local businessman blew-up all over us. He owned the local ice-cream shop, and I went to school with his daughter. This was going to be awkward.

I remember how mom and Al fought all night when he learned of her affair. He slammed out of the house pre-dawn and told her she had better be gone when he came back.

Her Prince Charmless came and loaded up his car with everything she could gather, including us. I had no idea where we were going, and I'm not sure she did either.

"I found you a great little place," he said. "It's only temporary but, you and the kids will be fine."

I looked at the back of his large head as he sat behind the wheel. His name was Jack. He was much larger than Al and had a wide, pockmarked face. What in the world did she see in this guy?

"What about school?" I asked.

"I'm sure there will be one," mom said sarcastically.

I was in sixth grade, and this would be my seventh school. I suppose I should have been used to it, but you never get used to perpetually being the new kid.

As I looked out the car window, the landscape became darker and seedier, like coal dust had enveloped everything. Where in hell were we going? Suddenly we pulled into a parking lot in front of a truck stop.

"You wait here, I'll go get the keys," Prince Charmless said.

As I looked around, I could see a trailer park behind the building. It could not have been uglier. It was October, and there was not a speck of fall color anywhere around us.

He came back with the keys, and we drove behind the building onto a gravel road lined with rusted out shitty tin boxes. One uglier than the next. My heart sank, and I wanted to cry.

"I know it doesn't look pretty but, as I said, it's temporary," he said.

"God, I hope so," I mumbled.

"You shut up!" mom yelled, "Jack's doing us a big favor after Al threw us out. You should be grateful we have a place to go."

"Why can't we go to Mamaw and Granddaddy's?" I asked.

"Don't you worry about it," she said, "we'll be fine."

My grandparents had always been there for us, even when they didn't agree with mom's way of handling the men in her life or how she treated her kids. I always felt safe with them and couldn't understand why she was keeping them away this time.

Barbara Hammond

The car stopped in front of a black and silver trailer with so much rust it resembled a calico cat. Jack got out and continued to assure her this was temporary.

"It's completely furnished," he said.

Mom nodded and followed him up the rickety wooden steps to the door.

"Come on, bring David and get in here," she said.

The outside was depressing enough but, the inside was complete with the smell of cat piss. It kept getting worse. How could this be happening?

He began describing it like he was trying to sell it, which he was. Not that she had a choice in the matter. There was no plan B.

"You can put the kid down," he said, "let him explore a little."

I was afraid of what he might find. Whoever lived there last must have left in a hurry because there were dirty dishes in the sink. I put David down and said, "Don't touch anything!"

"It needs a little cleaning," mom said. That was the understatement of the year.

"Let's unpack the car and then I'll take you to the store to get some food and cleaning supplies," he said.

They dropped our meager belongings inside the door and went shopping, leaving us there in the stinking tin box.

Daddy duJour

There was a small TV in the living room and, fortunately, it worked. I sat David in front of it and began looking through the cabinets for something to clean with.

The kitchen was tiny with a counter dividing it from the living room and a fold down table below a small window opposite the sink. There was a hallway down the side. The first bedroom had bunk beds where David and I would sleep, then a tiny bathroom and the (ahem) master bedroom taking the entire width of the back of the trailer.

I found a can of cleanser under the sink, filled a bowl with hot water and took a diaper out of the diaper bag to begin scrubbing things down.

I put all of the dishes in the sink. There weren't many, and they were all plastic with a sticky film on them. It was warm outside so opening the windows helped air things out. Everything I could clean I did. But, where the hell were they with the groceries?

By dusk, they returned. Clearly, they'd stopped at a bar.

"Hey! We brought food and new sheets for the beds," mom said.

For some reason, I thought he would be leaving. I was wrong. He brought in his own suitcase and took it to the back bedroom.

By November Prince Charmless was gone. Our temporary arrangement became permanent without any assistance. Mom got a job bartending 3pm-11pm. She made arrangements with an elderly neighbor woman to watch David until I got home from school around 3:30pm.

Sometimes mom would work a double shift at the bar, and I would have to stay home from school to babysit. My attendance record was pathetic but, I loved school and worked really hard to keep up.

"Are you all right back there, Miss?" The taxi driver asked.

"We're fine, thanks," I replied.

"I'm going to stop for gas up here," he said.

"Ok."

"Would you like me to get you a candy bar or pop?" he asked.

"How much longer before we get there?" I asked.

"Maybe 20 minutes or so," he replied.

"No, thanks, I'll be fine till we get there," I said.

David woke up. He stretched and rubbed his eyes as he looked around.

"I bet you're wondering where we are, aren't you buddy?"

He nodded and put his arms around my neck.

"We're going to aunt Lora and uncle Marvin's house!" I said, trying to sound excited about it.

Somehow, after Thanksgiving, Al's brother-in-law, Marvin, had discovered where we were. I heard a knock

Daddy duJour

on our door and was shocked to see Marvin there. He was a tall, burly kind of guy with a bald head and lots of freckles. I invited him in. He said he'd talked to mom and she said it was ok for us to go out to their house for the weekend. That was fine with me. I didn't even question him.

It became a regular thing for us, and I looked forward to it. By January we were planning to make it a permanent move to Waterville, Ohio, for David and me.

"Ok, we're full-up and back on our way," the driver said.

As we pulled away, I went back to thinking about the events that led up to this night.

Christmas had been beyond forgettable. I was grateful David was too young ever to remember it.

It was difficult to put on an act at school so people would think I was in the spirit of the season. Mom became suspicious of Lora around mid-December and refused to let us go to Waterville over the holiday. They never really liked each other but, I had no idea why.

Mom came home early from work drunk and dragged in a Charlie Brown tree she'd gotten at the lot up the road. They must have given her the tinsel and few lights that were on it since it was Christmas Eve.

She had stopped at the market and picked up a few apples and a bag of mixed nuts to go with the take-out sandwiches she'd brought from the bar where she worked. Hardly a Norman Rockwell Christmas scene.

We had a snowstorm daily, it seemed, and even trudging through from the back of the trailer park to the school bus was exhausting. But, the biggest issue with this wicked winter was running out of oil all the time.

We had no phone, so I had to use the one at the market across the street. If the oil ran out while mom was at work and the market was closed, we had to turn on the stove and hope the gas didn't run out.

I asked mom to get an electric heater for those times but, she said the electric bill was too high already, plus she said they were dangerous. Like leaving your kids alone without heat or with an open gas stove wouldn't be a danger to them.

One night the main water pipe into the kitchen froze. Having no clue what to do about it, I went to the elderly couple next door and asked if they knew what to do. He told me he had an electric heat wrap you could wrap around the pipe but, he couldn't help me do it.

"I can't crawl under there anymore, I'm sorry," he said, "but, I can loan it to you to try."

If the pipe burst we'd be in really bad shape so I said, "Sure I'll try."

He came out to point me in the right direction and walk me through it.

"First, you have to plug it in and run it out the kitchen window," he said.

Daddy duJour

So I went inside and plugged it in next to the kitchen window and rolled it out from there. It looked like a flat garden hose.

"I got it," he said.

Then I went outside and crawled underneath the trailer to find the pipe.

"You can't miss it," he said, "it's directly underneath in line with the window."

He had been kind enough to help me shovel out the snow a little bit so I could see what I was doing while he shined a flashlight.

"I got it," I said.

It was already getting hot, so I wrapped fast and secured the end.

"Now what?" I asked.

"That's it," he said. "It should thaw it out soon enough, and you'll be fine."

"Do I leave it on all night?" I asked.

"You better," he said.

I was frozen to the bone, but I felt pretty damn proud of myself. Now, if the gas didn't run out, we would be fine.

We made it through the night. In the morning I heard the oil truck coming through the trailer park as I was getting ready for school. Mom was asleep, so I flagged him down. At least, we'd be warm for a week or so. Oil wasn't lasting as long as it should because we were at negative temperatures most of the time.

Mom's latest flame was obnoxious. Whenever there was a new one she would rave about how wonderful he was and warn me to be nice to him. I tried but, Bruce was a pompous ass. I think she assumed he was smart because he acted so arrogantly and used big words.

He had beady eyes and a big hook nose that held up his thick horn-rimmed glasses. His hair was dark and thick slicked back with too much pomade. He gave me the creeps.

One night he came to take mom out. While she was finishing getting dressed he thought it would be a good time to give me some pointers about dating.

"In a couple of years you'll be dating," he said. "Maybe you'll be asked to the prom, which is a big extravagant dance, and your date will take you out to dinner at a fancy restaurant."

I'm thinking, oh dear God, where is this going.

"When it's a big important evening like that you must order the most expensive item on the menu," he said.

"What if I don't like the most expensive item on the menu?" I asked.

"It doesn't matter," he said, "you order it anyway because it's expected."

"That's ridiculous," I said.

Daddy duJour

Thankfully mom was ready to go, and the lesson was ended. I shook it off and hoped he wouldn't be hanging around much longer.

The next week he came home with mom and said he was going to take me to dinner to show me how I should act on a date. Mom thought this was a good idea. I certainly did not!

His idea of a fancy restaurant was the steakhouse on the road in front of the trailer park. Not exactly the Ritz. They did, however, have lobster, and he insisted I order the surf and turf. He had no idea, apparently, that the dish in front of me was more food than I normally consumed in a week.

I couldn't finish it, and while he was paying the tab, I slipped out and started walking back to the trailer. He also went back to the trailer, bringing my doggie bag and telling mom what an ungrateful bitch I was.

A week later we were out of oil again, and it was twenty below zero. I made it to the market before closing time and called mom.

"Why are you bothering me at work?" she screamed.

"We're out of oil, and it's freezing, and I'm afraid the gas won't last either," I yelled back.

"Bruce is giving me a ride home, and we'll stop and get a tank of gas," she said. "Now don't call me again."

By 11pm, we were out of gas. If she came home right after her shift we would probably be ok, I thought. In the meantime, I gathered every blanket, bedspread, coat and even towels, to bury the two of us under while we waited for her to get home.

They showed up around 1am, drunk.

When she walked in and saw us, she said, "Shit! We forgot to get the gas."

She looked at me and knew I really wanted to kill her at that moment.

"It's ok," he said, "we'll go get it now."

They got back in the car and left us there while they went to get gas. I was terrified they wouldn't come back. But, if anger is fuel, I would get through the night.

They did make it back in a relatively short time and got the stove going. Bruce left without a word. Mom passed out in the chair across from us.

"I have to do the early shift today, so you have to stay home," were her first words the next morning.

Then she took a shower and got dressed as I fed David his breakfast. Not another word was spoken until she was ready to leave.

"I'll see you tonight," she said.

"No, you won't," I replied.

She looked at me curiously and walked out the door.

Chapter II

Marvin and Lora

"We're here, young lady," the taxi driver said.

I looked up and saw Al coming toward the taxi with his sister, Lora. David ran to his dad, and we all hugged. I was a jumble of feelings. Somewhere between relieved and tied in knots. We had been here many times but, never like this. There was no way to know what would happen next.

Al had been my step-dad since I was five. Mom and my father divorced when I was two. Her second husband is another story altogether. We'll get to him later. Mom was on her third husband at the ripe old age of twenty-two. I was an only child for nine years, and I enjoyed it.

Al was about 5'9" with sandy blonde hair and baby blue eyes. He was twenty-five when they married. He had worked as a mechanic at times before he got a factory job.

Mom was laid off after a year at the factory and Al a few months later. Money was tight, and the arguments were loud and frequent. She took a part-time job waitressing at the bowling alley lounge.

Being young, petite and very attractive mom got a lot of attention. She wasn't shy about flirting, and Al didn't like it one little bit. He would leave me alone after I went to bed at night to go watch her at the bar. They always woke me up when they came home arguing at 2 am.

Eventually, Al was back at the factory but, mom decided to keep the waitressing gig. She loved all the attention. Things were tense for quite a while until she discovered she was pregnant. I don't believe it was planned, but they both seemed happy about it.

On October 21, 1959, two months prematurely, mom delivered a baby boy. He was so tiny they brought him home in doll clothes. She had him cesarean section, as she had me, and she was determined to stretch the recovery time as long as possible. It didn't faze Al at all. He seemed to revel in taking care of the baby and me.

I quickly learned how to change diapers and handle feedings. I wasn't very big myself, for a nine-year-old but definitely mature for my age. Before long I was the primary caregiver because mom had to go back to work. The bowling alley lounge was the only opportunity for her.

Al was living in constant jealousy. He sat in the bowling alley lounge most nights watching her and then berating her flirting behavior. Before long there was no peace at home and mom decided to leave Al. It would be their first of several separations.

David and I made the first big step, getting to Waterville, that cold January night but, I still wasn't sure what would come next. Knowing mom would be really pissed and obstruct us any and every way she could, made me uneasy.

"Let's get you inside where it's warm," Lora said.

She got no argument from me. I felt like Scarlett O'Hara in Gone with the Wind when she grabbed the potato out of the dirt and with her fist up to God declared, "As God is my witness, I will never go hungry again!"

My declaration was never to be freezing cold again. And, walking into their warm and cozy home was emotional for me. I bit my lip to keep from crying because my armor was still up. There was no guarantee this would work out.

Lora had made chili-mac for dinner, and I gorged myself on it. David even ate more than he usually did. Maybe he would gain some weight now, I thought. Both of us were underweight, and it was as much from stress as lack of good food in my case.

Marvin and Lora's son, whom they called Buttons, was five years old. He was a cute freckle-faced kid. I felt he was a little uncertain about having us moving in with them. So was I.

After dinner, Lora showed me to my room. She was a petite little blonde. There was a definite resemblance to her brother, Al. They were both fair skinned, with thin frames.

Her husband, Marvin almost seemed too large next to her. He worked in construction and was tall, bald and beefy.

It was a small house that backed up to the Maumee River. The front of the house faced the road and looked like a ranch style. Outside were cement steps on either side of the house leading down a rather steep hill and out to the river. Underneath the house was a basement with a door and windows facing the river. It was primarily used for storage.

They had taken their sun porch and turned it into my room. It was small and had lots of windows with lacy curtains on them. She had thought to put shades as well, for privacy. I appreciated that since it faced the street. The room had a twin bed and a small dresser with a chair next to it.

David would be sleeping in Buttons' room, and they had gotten him a small bed with rails on the side. Even though we had a room in the trailer with bunk beds, most nights we would be together on the couch because the stove was on for warmth. But, sometimes, it was to get away from the noises in mom's room.

It took a few nights before David slept through the night in his new bed in Button's room. He would crawl in with me, and I was always happy to have him with me. We were in this together, and he was as much comfort to me as I to him.

Our first day there Lora took me shopping for new school clothes. I was probably an embarrassment to her with the clothes I'd brought with me. She wanted a more Bobby Brooks style than anything I owned. I certainly didn't disagree or object.

Daddy duJour

We chose a couple of pleated wool skirts in pastel colors, with sweaters to mix and match. It was the pale pink skirt that bore the stain of my first period. Damn, the curse began in earnest.

Chapter

III

Minnie and Delmar

Marvin and Lora's home was lovely and warm but, nothing as special as the home I stayed in for six months when I was five.

My mother married Al the year I turned five. I liked him very much. They met at the factory where they worked. We lived in a small 1-bedroom apartment over a garage in town. I'd slept on the pullout sofa since he moved in.

Kindergarten wasn't required back then. There wasn't even a kindergarten class available in the public school we lived near. I was an avid fan of books, Captain Kangaroo, and The Mickey Mouse Club. I knew about school and couldn't wait until I was old enough to go. It was disappointing having to wait another year.

Then something wonderful happened. Mom and Al were switched to 3rd shift. Working 11pm to 7am meant taking care of a 5-year-old was going to be a problem. I recall lots of discussion about what to do with the kid.

I don't remember many of the details, but this became life altering for me. Apparently, my great aunt Barb's sister-in-law and husband, who were probably in their 60's, offered to take me in. I had never met them, and neither had my mother.

Daddy duJour

I loved aunt Barb, who I was named after. She was Mamaw's youngest sister. We didn't get to see each other often since she lived in Georgia, but whenever she was around it was fun. Everyone agreed it would be fine to move me out to the country. It was one move I have never regretted.

There was a bit of culture shock when I first arrived. The yard was open and green. I had never had a big yard to play in. Even my grandparents lived in the city then. Minnie and Delmar's house was beautiful, inside and out. I was afraid to touch anything. It wasn't palatial by any means, but so pristinely inviting.

There was a vase of flowers on the kitchen table. They must have come from the beautiful flower garden I'd seen next to their driveway. I could smell fresh coffee and the wonderful aroma of warm muffins. A clock on the living room mantle startled me when it chimed on the hour. I grew to love that chime.

It took me about two seconds to fall in love with my bedroom. It was the most beautiful bedroom I had ever seen, and it was mine alone. The house was a Cape Cod style, and my room was up under the eaves. The ceiling sloped on both sides, and there was a nice sized window at each end.

There were twin beds, so I alternated beds for a while until Minnie told me I had to choose one because she wasn't interested in washing extra sheets each week. I complied.

The biggest shock was my first breakfast there. I was used to making my own cereal or just sitting in front of the TV eating dry cereal out of the box. My mother wasn't a morning person, and that never bothered me.

I woke the first morning to the smell of coffee and something else that made me salivate… was it pancakes? I ran downstairs and stopped dead at the kitchen door.

The table was dressed in a pale yellow cloth, beautiful flowers were in a vase at the center of the table, and there were 3 place settings. Each place had a small glass of orange juice, a plate, silverware and a cloth napkin. Wow. I'd only seen something like that on TV.

Minnie was humming at the stove, Delmar, was sitting at the table holding a chair out for me. I haltingly walked in and sat down. Was I dreaming? The entire scenario was a beautiful assault on my senses.

The only problem was the missing coffee cup from my place at the table. When I asked for one, they were shocked.

"Oh honey, you're much too young for coffee!" Minnie said.

I informed her that I'd been drinking coffee since I was 2 years old and would truly love a cup right then. She wasn't going to relent, but Delmar gave her a little nod, and she asked me what I'd like in it. I showed her how my grandmother fixed it for me. She relaxed a bit when she realized my idea of coffee was primarily coffee flavored sugary milk.

Daddy duJour

I sat down next to Delmar and waited for the pancakes. I watched him place his napkin on his lap and did the same. I'd never used cloth napkins before. Then Minnie brought a large plate of pancakes and sat them on the table. I wanted to reach for the pancakes, but I waited.

They bowed their heads and gave thanks to the Lord for the meal. I did the same, and we all said, 'Amen.' Then she took my plate and asked how many pancakes I would like. I asked for two even though I was pretty sure I could eat more I didn't want to seem rude. She assured me I could have more.

As I stuffed my face with pancakes, Minnie told me they were going to get me registered for kindergarten that day. Then I knew I must be dreaming!

"REALLY?" I screamed.

This was amazing to me. You can't imagine the sheer joy I experienced in less than 48hrs. I was on cloud nine!

The kindergarten was in a two-room little house in the back of a larger elementary school. There was a playground between them, and we had our own separate time to use it, right before nap time. I had never been good at napping but, after the fresh air and outdoor games, I learned to enjoy it.

We only had half-days, but they were packed with fun things to do. I loved the coloring time and music, too.

Minnie would walk me to school in the morning and would be waiting for me when the bell rang. We would talk about my day and hers, too, on the walk home.

Sometimes we would stop to visit with her neighbor, Sally, who was quite a bit older than Minnie. Her house was very cluttered and stuffy, but the smell of fresh baked cookies always drew me in.

The six months spent with those lovely people made such an impression on me. It was impossible not to compare what I'd known and what could be. They gave me hope for a better life, a standard to aspire to. I am forever grateful for them.

I was able to visit them occasionally after I left. It was always a pleasure. I believe they gave me my love for flowers, as well as the desire always to make my home warm and inviting.

Chapter

IV

Going to Court

After being in Waterville for a couple of weeks, I found out we were going to court. Lora told me mom hadn't even bothered to contact them, but suddenly she was taking them to court accusing them of abducting her children. I didn't know what to expect.

We went into a large office building in downtown Toledo and waited in a hallway. I sat between Lora and Marvin on a long bench. My stomach was in knots because I expected mom to be there. She was not.

I was escorted into an office and introduced to an older man, who seemed friendly enough. He said we would just talk for a while about our leaving mom.

"What do you want to know?" I asked.

"Can you tell me why you chose to go to your stepfather's sister?" he asked.

"She wanted us," I replied.

"But, she has no legal right to take you and your brother away from your mother," he said.

"But Al does," I said.

He pulled some papers out of his desk and showed me where the court had denied Al custody when they divorced. I was surprised and not sure I believed him.

"But, we're not living with Al," I said, "Lora and Marvin can adopt us."

"Why would you want to hurt your mother?" he asked.

"Hurt *her*?" I asked.

"She is devastated by your actions," he said.

Aha! She had this guy wrapped around her finger. I had to set the record straight.

"Did she tell you about leaving us to freeze on one of the coldest nights on record while she was out drinking with her new boyfriend?" I asked. "I'm sure you haven't heard everything if you believe her story," I said.

He held up his hand to stop me and said, "Your mother loves you and..."

"No," I said, "no she doesn't. She is looking for your sympathy so she can hurt my step-father," I said.

"We're pieces in a game to her, she doesn't care about us, or she wouldn't have left us to freeze in horrible conditions with barely any food half the time," I said.

He kept trying to make me feel sorry for her, and it only made me more furious. I wished she had been there because I really wanted to choke her. Instead, I told him how we ended up in the horrible trailer and then were left there when her ex-boyfriend was done with her. I told him how embarrassing it was to be her daughter. I emptied my gut in hopes of a little understanding.

He listened for a while then asked if I wanted a glass of water or a soda. I was thirsty and in knots after spewing to this guy and feeling it was time wasted. I agreed a break would be good. He left the room and returned quickly with a bottle of Pepsi and a small bag of pretzels.

"I have to make a short appearance in court and thought you might like a snack, too," he said. "I won't be long so, please relax, and we will continue our talk when I get back."

His office was dark wood with only an ornate lamp on the desk. The Venetian blinds were cracked open a bit, and sunlight streamed in highlighting the dust on his credenza. There were tarnished silver candlesticks that seemed oddly out of place.

His desk chair was large and covered in red velvet. How odd, I thought. There were no pictures only tchotchkes that reminded me of an old spinster like Miss Havisham from Great Expectations.

I loved reading, and Dickens was one of my favorites. My reading level had been high from the second grade. I'm sure it was due to the times I had been alone with David and had no TV. In hindsight, that was a blessing.

I expected Havisham would ask me about the afternoon I left David alone in the trailer with the stove on. It was the first time, that freezing cold winter, I was tempted to be a kid and play in the snow.

It seemed there was a fresh inch or two of snow daily and lots of kids in the trailer park would be out having snowball fights or building snowmen. One day, as I got off the school bus, a girl asked me if I could come to join them build a snow fort. I of course declined.

David didn't have a decent snowsuit, and he didn't have boots. I couldn't leave him alone while I ran out to play.

But, the girl came over a while later and convinced me, if we stayed within David's view he could watch, and I could keep an eye on him. That seemed reasonable to my twelve-year-old mind.

The next thing I knew I had wandered away from our trailer and the booming voice of my grandfather was echoing through the trailer park.

"Barbara Jean!"

Oh my God! I was frightened and excited all at once. We hadn't seen our grandparents since we had been in this awful place. I knew mom had kept it a secret, but when Marvin had discovered where we were the cat was out of the bag.

I followed the booming voice and saw him standing in front of our trailer. He looked angry but, he gave me a long and suffocating hug and, it felt so good. I could tell he wasn't happy with our living arrangements.

"Girl, you can't go off and leave this baby alone with the stove on!" He said.

"I didn't mean to get away from the trailer but..."

"Why is the stove on anyway?" he asked.

"We keep running out of oil, and if they don't get here with a new tank before 5pm, we have to wait till morning and the stove is all we have for heat," I explained.

"You stay here with David. I'm going over to make a call," he said.

Granddaddy came back with some soup and a loaf of bread, peanut butter, and jelly, too. Apparently, he'd looked through the cupboards. He hung around for a while to make sure we ate and were tucked in for the night. He made me promise to never leave David alone again and to call him if I needed anything.

It was the day after Granddaddy's visit I met mom's version of child care.

I saw my mother sleeping on the couch. I started to make breakfast for David, and she woke up.

"So... you contacted your grandfather, huh?" Were her first words of the day.

"Me?" I asked. "I didn't call him. I thought you did."

"Sure, I wanted him to walk into my bar and rip me a new asshole in front of everybody. All over your stupidity." She yelled while moving closer.

"Hey, I was shocked to see him, but I was really happy he got us some oil. It was freezing cold last night. I was afraid we'd run out of gas, too. But you wouldn't care about that would you?" I responded as I kept fixing David's cereal.

She jerked me around to face her, and I saw contempt and weariness in her eyes. Knowing she couldn't fight her father, now that he knew where she'd been hiding out, she was resigned to it. I believe she was actually relieved. I have no idea what she thought her life was going to be when she ran off with her Prince Charmless, but I'm sure she didn't envision anything quite this seedy and depressing.

Now she could surrender and hope her parents would take care of her kids, like they'd done many times in the past, and leave her alone. I believe she never really wanted either of us and had never taken responsibility anyway, so now she could stop pretending. That's what I was hoping as I made my way to the bus stop.

I was in such a good mood all day. Surely granddaddy would be back to get us. He wouldn't let us stay in this hell hole, would he? Even if he felt we should stay with mom, I knew Mamaw would have a fit when she heard about our living conditions. She would make him come to rescue us.

My mind wandered all day and even more so during the bus ride home. I just knew things were going to get better now. They had to!

I stopped at our neighbor's trailer to get David, and the lady said our new babysitter had taken him to our trailer. I didn't understand what she was talking about.

When I opened the door to the trailer, I saw three total strangers sitting on the couch.

"Who are YOU?" I demanded.

Daddy duJour

The woman sitting in the middle said, "We're here to babysit hon. Your mama called and asked us to take care of you while she works."

"How do you know my mother?"

"We know her from her work... well I do," she began, "My name's Mary by the way, and I wait tables there part-time, and she knew I was looking for more work. I don't drive so my dad here drove me over." She continued, "This is my brother Tom, he came along for the ride."

"We don't need a babysitter," I said, "I've been taking care of my brother for a very long time. You can leave now. We'll be fine."

"Oh no honey, you shouldn't be tending to a baby," she said.

I was mentally scrambling and trying to figure out how to make them leave. It was hard to think straight because what I wanted most was to find my mother and choke the life out of her. She didn't really know these people. She didn't care either.

It struck me that neither her father nor brother had mumbled a sound. They sat there slack-jawed gaping at me. It also struck me that they were all big and fat. How were we going to manage three huge extra people in this tiny place?

The thought had barely been formed when Mary said, "This trailer's a little cramped so we thought we'd take you two to our house."

"Honestly, we are perfectly fine here. Why don't you guys just head on home? I'll work this out with mom tomorrow." I was praying that would work but no... she was getting their coats, and I hadn't even taken mine off yet.

I pulled David away from her and wrapped him up. I couldn't fight three huge people so I was going to have to go along and work it out as I could. I had to stop the anger in my head and focus. These people weren't that bright, in my assessment, so I could figure out how to get away somehow.

As we all piled into the beat up old car that they'd parked at the tavern on their way in, I knew I had to pay attention to where we were going. I had a pretty good sense of direction and had lived in many areas of town. This shouldn't be too difficult.

Before long I realized I had absolutely no idea where we were but it looked worse than the area our trailer was in. Suddenly we turned right onto a four-lane street with run down or boarded up businesses, then a sharp left and they stopped the car.

"Here we are!" Mary sang out as she opened the back door. I got out and looked around at seedy and dilapidated houses. Some had front porches, and some looked as if the porches had fallen off. The house we were walking up to had a porch, but it didn't look very sturdy.

Daddy duJour

If the outside was less than inviting the inside was worse. The smell was repulsive. I couldn't put my finger on exactly what the stench was, but I felt nauseous.

In this large boxy living room, there was only one lamp on, and it gave everything a dim and eerie feel. They had a TV and on the couch in front of it was a couple wrapped in a blanket together. They barely looked up as Mary introduced me to her other brother and his girlfriend.

"Follow me, hon, I'll fix you somethin' to eat," Mary said as she threw her coat on the back of a chair and headed toward the back of the house. I left my coat on. Nothing was going to stand in my way of escaping somehow. I explained to her I was always cold, which wasn't much of a stretch.

The kitchen was huge and filthy. The sink was full of dirty dishes, overflowing onto the counter next to it. There were pots on the stove with dried on chunks of God knows what and a dish rag hanging on the oven handle that was almost black it was so nasty.

As I was taking all of this in Mary began screaming at the top of her lungs. "Marty, goddamit I told you to do the dishes! Just because you didn't think we'd be back so quick, you decided to fuck your girl instead of doing what I told you. Get your sorry ass in here and start washin' 'em now!"

"It's ok, really, David's falling asleep, and I'm not hungry at all." I blurted out, "Where can I put him down?"

"I'll show you," She said as she led me back into the living room, smacked Marty on the back of the head, and then opened the door next to the TV.

I felt immediately assaulted by pink. I had never seen so much pink in one place in my life! This room didn't look girlie it looked like someone had spewed Pepto Bismol all over it.

I guessed Mary to be about twenty. There was nothing feminine about her at all so I thought there must be another girl in this bizarre family. As I was taking it all in she said, "You can put him down in my bed. This is the only clean room in the house."

"OK, thanks," I said as I laid him down in the middle of the ruffled bedspread. The pillows were covered with dolls dressed in frilly pink dresses. They had porcelain faces that seemed real. Everything about this place gave me the creeps. I had to get out of here!

She tossed me a blanket as she walked out of the room. I could hear her yelling obscenities at Marty and his girlfriend, who apparently hadn't gone in to do the dishes.

I laid there with David as he drifted off to sleep. I knew he was probably hungry, but he never cried. I was hungry too and really wanted to cry, but I had to keep my mind on getting the hell out of there.

I've always had a great memory for phone numbers. I can't remember names and I am terrible at math, but phone numbers stick in my head. I remembered seeing a phone booth on the four-lane street we'd turned off of and decided to call Al. Surely he would come and get us.

I dozed off for a while and when I woke it was very quiet, and I thought everyone had gone to sleep. There was a stream of light, from the street lamp, coming in through a hole in the pull-down window shade. I got up slowly hoping the bed wouldn't creak.

As I opened the bedroom door, I was so careful not to make a sound. The door creaked a bit, and I cringed. I peered out into the living room. Someone was sleeping on the couch, but I couldn't tell who. There was a light on in the kitchen but no noise.

The lump on the couch moved, and I could see it was Mary. It made sense since David and I were in her bed that she'd crash on the couch. I was hoping she was a sound sleeper. The clock on the wall above the TV said it was 10:23 pm. I had slept longer than I thought.

I slipped back into the bedroom, and as my eyes adjusted to the dim light, I could see the top of the dresser. There was a small dish with some loose change in it, and I took it all. Then I grabbed David, wrapped the blanket as snug around him as I could and tiptoed toward the door.

The front door wasn't locked, so that was easy. The creaking front steps were so loud I was afraid they would wake the entire neighborhood, but nothing stirred. I headed toward the main drag where the phone booth was.

I woke Al up when I called, but he came through for us. "Where exactly are you?" He asked, and I had no idea. He told me to give him the names on the street sign at the corner. When I did, he said, "I'll send a cab for you right away. It's going to be all right."

As I stood there inside the phone booth, to stay out of the wind, I felt relieved yet worried. What would happen now? Did mom know we would be taken some place else? Would it have mattered to her? Would she have come looking for us?

I was also feeling a little bit bad about sneaking away from Mary. She was just trying to make a buck babysitting. Clearly, she needed the money and, I could tell from her room that she wanted something better for her life just like I did.

"You haven't touched your soda," he said.

I was startled out of my ugly reverie by the attorney. I didn't even know his name, and he didn't have a nameplate on his desk. I began thinking of him as Havisham.

"We've had a brief meeting about where you should be living," Havisham said, "and, for now, the discussion you and I have had will be put on hold."

"What does that mean?" I asked.

"It means you can go home with the Smiths and we will meet again soon," he said.

Daddy duJour

Havisham held the door open, and Marvin and Lora were waiting in the hall. She looked quite pleased, and I thought, maybe things would work out for the best.

Once we were in the car, I asked what happened.

"It's really nothing for you to worry about, Barb," Lora said.

"But is it over? Will we be living with you guys now?" I had a million questions and wasn't completely sure I wanted all the answers. I wanted to simply relax into, what might be, our new home and family.

Chapter V

Michigan

When we returned to Marvin and Lora's house after seeing the attorney things seemed a little different. There were lively conversations in their bedroom I wasn't privy to, even though I knew it was about David and me.

I had adjusted to going back to school with kids I'd known before mom and Al split. Mom's Prince Charmless had left town with his family, so I didn't have to meet his daughter in the hallway. That was a relief.

By early spring, we seemed to be in a comfortable routine. I knew Lora didn't do this for me. I knew she wanted custody of David because she'd always wanted another child and it never happened. She wasn't mean to me in any way, but we weren't warm and friendly either. Had her plan to separate David and me worked, we would have had major issues.

One Saturday morning she announced we were going for a ride. When I asked where she said, "You'll see."

We were heading north on the highway. I couldn't imagine where we could be going on such a damp and dreary day. Looking out the window, everything looked gray and foreboding. Then I saw a sign…

Daddy duJour

Welcome to Michigan!

"What are we doing in Michigan?" I asked.

"We're going to meet with your dad," Lora said.

"Why?"

"You'll see," she said.

I hadn't seen my father in two years. It wasn't a good experience the last time. Why in hell were we going to see him now? My stomach flipped.

I remembered living in an ugly and depressing apartment with mom after she and Al separated the first time. David wasn't quite walking yet but, very active. A neighbor would sit with him when mom left for her job bartending around noon while I was in school, then the sitter would leave when I got home.

I usually made dinner from a box or can, and we'd watch TV after. He was starting to stand and toddle around a bit holding onto furniture, but there was not much stimulation for either of us.

One evening there was a knock at the door, and it startled me. We never had company. Mom had a key and wouldn't be home for a few more hours. I put the chain on the door and slowly peeked out.

A man holding a bag of groceries said, "Aren't you going to let your dear old dad in?"

I hadn't seen him in so long I didn't recognize him. He was tall dark and handsome, couldn't deny it. He had dark blue eyes, and I wished I'd inherited them instead of brown.

"Your mom told me to pick up some groceries," he said, "she'll be here in a little while."

I let him in.

"Can't you give your old dad a hug?" he asked.

I didn't move. He wrapped his arm around me, and I froze. 'Who the hell does he think he is,' was running through my head.

He proceeded to the kitchen to put the groceries away and informed me we had roaches.

"I know," I said.

Mom came home, and they made dinner. I don't remember much of it. My mind was in a constant loop around 'why is he here?'

It was a one-bedroom apartment but, there was a murphy bed in the living room. After dinner, I sat down in the living room to do homework. Mom suggested I should take it into the kitchen or bedroom so they could talk. I went into the bedroom because I knew the roaches preferred the kitchen.

I could hear them talking but couldn't make out what they were saying. After a while it got quiet, and I went out to find them making out in a chair.

"Don't look at me like that," she said, "we were married you know?"

Daddy duJour

I didn't say anything. She told me to get ready for bed and, "You can have the bed all to yourself because I'm sleeping out here with your daddy."

I went and brushed my teeth and put my pajamas on. They had elastic around the legs and when I came out to say goodnight the two of them started laughing at me.

"Look!" mom said, "She must be afraid a roach will crawl up into her coochie."

I was humiliated and totally pissed off. I turned and walked away, got into bed and cried. I didn't sleep much because the bed I was in was up against the wall of the Murphy bed which was rocking quite a bit.

By the third day of having him around the why became clear. His wife had thrown him out for cheating with my mother! I don't know how long they had been seeing each other but obviously longer than the three days he'd been living in our apartment.

On the third night, I overheard them talking about his other daughter, who was four years younger than me. Dad said she was sick and the wife wanted him to come home and help her take care of the girl. It didn't go over well with mom.

The end of the week rolled around, and dad moved back to his wife and young daughter in Michigan.

"Are you happy now?" mom screamed as she slammed the door.

"What are you talking about?" I asked.

"You couldn't be nice to him, so he went back to that bitch and her daughter!" she screamed.

"Why is that my fault?" I asked.

"You never were sweet to him. He kept trying to be nice to you, but you didn't care. Now look what you've done!" she sobbed.

I had no response. As far as I was concerned, he was nothing to me.

I don't know the reason my parents split up after barely two years of marriage but the fact that they were seventeen and twenty with each having only a tenth-grade education when they married probably had a lot to do with it.

I've also learned, over the years, they are both narcissists. Narcissism is not a great trait for a parent.

Lora pulled into a gravel driveway next to a small white house. There was a young girl playing in the front yard looking at us curiously. The weather was gray and my memory of this day in my life will forever be in black and white.

From everything I had heard from my mother, I expected the step-mother, Betty, to have a pointed hat and warts on her nose. In fact, she was a petite blonde woman who seemed very sweet.

We went into the kitchen where she had prepared coffee and cake. I looked around but saw no signs of my dad. We all sat around the kitchen table except the little girl who was still outside playing in the drizzle.

Daddy duJour

"Your dad took a job driving truck," Betty said, "He couldn't be here today but, we both agree you should be living with us."

You could have knocked me over with a feather. What the hell were they thinking? Whose idea was this? My head was exploding!

"I don't think that's a good idea," I said.

"Give her a chance to explain, Barb," Lora said.

"What's to explain?" I asked.

"We can't get custody of you, and they can't get custody of David," Lora said, "so the best thing is for you to live with your dad and we can adopt David," Lora explained.

"Do my grandparents know about this?" I asked.

"I don't know," Betty said.

"I know I've taken better care of David than our mom and still he misses her. If you take me out of his life, he will be totally confused. It can't be good for him," I said.

"You're too young to be raising a child, Barb," Betty said. "If you live with us you can be a kid like it should be."

"I can't unwind my life to give all of you what you want," I said. "My father doesn't want me, he chose your daughter over me, Betty," I said.

"I know you don't want me, Lora, you only want David," I said. "But I can't walk away from my brother. How could you ask me to?"

I was visibly shaken and dying inside. I was aware if push came to shove. I wouldn't have a leg to stand on in court. Twelve-year-old girls aren't taken seriously as guardians but, that's the role I'd lived for two years. How could they do this to David and me?

"I want to talk to my grandparents," I said.

I don't remember much of the conversation after that. They bantered about whether my grandparents would have a say in their scheme and I tuned out. The shock had overtaken me, and I was desperately trying not to cry. If they saw a weakness they would pounce, I knew it.

We drove back to Waterville in the gray drizzle. The weather suited my mood perfectly. The sky was crying for me.

Chapter

VI

Mamaw and Granddaddy

This is my version of the stories I heard throughout my childhood about my Grandparents life before they moved North. I suppose it could be considered Historical Fiction or Family Lore. I include it for a broader perspective of the family and how it evolved. When I think of the stories about Granddaddy's whoopings, I feel like he viewed me as his redemption.

My grandmother, who I've always called Mamaw had known Grady, my Grandfather, her entire life. The day she was born, on a cotton farm in rural Georgia, he and his mother walked up the road from their farm to see the new baby. He was six years old.

By the time Mamaw was fourteen, it was simply a foregone conclusion they would marry. Marrying at fourteen was not uncommon for a girl in 1926, especially in the rural South. Granddaddy was doing quite well for a young man of twenty. He was hard working and smart, despite not finishing school.

Granddaddy's oldest brother, Lawrence, had taken over running the family farm when their father passed away, and that was fine with him. He never felt he was meant to be a farmer. He was good with his hands and had started helping a local carpenter when he was only ten.

The year they married, Granddaddy became a Southern Baptist Minister, in addition to working as a carpenter. He was a very devout servant of the church and expected his wife to follow his lead. Mamaw's family was Methodist, but she gladly changed her affiliation because she felt her job, as a wife, was to be loyal to her husband.

Their first child, Ruby, was born nine months after they married. Being she was the only child, she had her mother's undivided attention. Granddaddy wasn't home very much. Between his carpentry work and being a Deacon at their church, he was a very busy man. His only role in child rearing, as he saw it, was to be the provider and disciplinarian. He was quite serious about both.

Mamaw had a son, Charles, 2 months after Ruby's 4th birthday. She'd gotten pregnant again almost immediately after having Charles. There were problems with this pregnancy she hadn't experienced with the others. She miscarried at four months.

With Granddaddy's strict religious beliefs, he would have no mourning over something that was 'God's Will' in his home. Even though Mamaw was devastated by the loss, she put on a brave face for him and mourned alone in silence.

Ruby was saddened over the loss, as well. She had asked Mamaw a lot of questions about the pregnancy and was looking forward to a new brother or sister. It was difficult to explain to a five-year-old when she didn't understand it herself.

Daddy duJour

When she got pregnant again, within a few months, Mamaw tried to be more aware of her physical limitations. She didn't want to lose this one. Her sister, Dotty, was more than happy to help out.

Dotty was a year younger than Mamaw. She'd been married for 2 years, and had no children of her own, despite wanting them more than anything. She loved her sister's kids as her own. It was a Godsend that Dotty lived close by, for both of them.

They had settled in a small town several miles from their families' farms. It seemed like a big city to Mamaw. New homes were popping up all the time, which provided a steady stream of work for Granddaddy and a growing community to raise their family.

A daughter, Joanne, arrived in June. She was one month early, but everyone seemed healthy. Ruby and Charles were so excited about the baby they couldn't take their eyes off her. Charles was very protective of Joanne. It was as if he sensed she was fragile.

Granddaddy had built another room onto their little house before Joanne arrived. It became Charles' bedroom, so the girls could share one. Mamaw would've kept the baby in their bedroom, but Granddaddy wouldn't allow it. It didn't matter to him that it was more difficult for feedings in the night, or that Mamaw was almost fearful of letting Joanne out of her sight. He made the rules of the house, and one of them was children should not be allowed in their parent's bedroom. Most mornings he would find Mamaw asleep, in the rocking chair she had placed in the girl's room, holding the baby.

Joanne slept a lot more than her first two children, and Mamaw considered this a blessing because her days were very hectic now with three to care for. She would find herself forgetting the baby was even in the house sometimes because she napped so much. It didn't seem unusual to her that Joanne was still sleeping when Granddaddy came home for dinner, that night in October, even though she had gone down for her nap three hours earlier.

Everyone gathered at the table for supper as Mamaw went to get the baby. She thought Joanne felt cold at first touch and blamed herself for being too busy to check earlier and put another blanket on her. It was getting cooler now that fall had arrived. As she leaned down to lift the baby out of the crib reality came over her in waves, and she passed out.

She woke up in her own bed, with Dotty sitting next to her.

"What happened?" Mamaw asked.

"You just got a little woozy, honey. You're gonna be just fine, though." Dotty said.

Mamaw knew that was a lie. She was very groggy, but she knew her baby was dead and she was not going to be all right.

"How long have I been sleeping?" she asked.

"The Dr. came and gave you some medicine because you were pretty sick and you've been resting for a day or so," Dotty said.

Daddy duJour

"A day or so?" she screamed.

She tried to get up but couldn't. She was so dizzy, and her head was pounding as she blacked out again.

Granddaddy arranged the funeral. Mamaw was unable to leave her bed. She went from sobbing uncontrollably to staring intently at the ceiling as if her gaze could penetrate clear through to God, who she desperately wanted an answer from.

After baby Joanne's funeral, Granddaddy went back to the house. He was worried about Mamaw even if he didn't show it. A man wasn't supposed to show emotion, he had to be strong. This was God's will, and he accepted it as such. He knew Mamaw couldn't handle it emotionally and he needed her to understand they were helpless to change any of it.

Mamaw was in no condition to get out of bed, let alone listen to Granddaddy's preaching. Her depression was palpable. Her sister, Dotty, intended to take care of Ruby and Charles as long as she was needed. She and Eugene wanted children so desperately this felt like their own loss. She mourned every month when she realized she wasn't pregnant. The pain of having a child and losing it months later was incomprehensible to her.

Betty, my mother, was born May 6th, 1933, a year after Joanne's death. Ruby was in school full-time, and Charles was at Dottie's, more often than not. Even though this left Mamaw and her baby alone most of the day, she couldn't seem to bond with her.

This was the most vocal and difficult child she'd ever known. Nothing seemed to make her happy. She rejected her mother's breast, which meant trying other means of nourishment.

Baby formula wasn't widely used in rural Georgia then. Mamaw experimented with powdered milk. She couldn't seem to find a consistency to satisfy Betty. Finally, she resorted to adding a bit of Karo syrup to the mix. That worked. It worked for me, too, seventeen years later.

Granddaddy had planted quite a substantial garden early that spring. Since then he had taken on several odd jobs, which left Mamaw to tend the garden. It was a typical hot and humid summer that year, and an unhappy infant didn't make it more tolerable.

As Betty became accustomed to her bottle, Mamaw began to add solids to her diet. She believed it was hunger that made the baby so irritable, and she couldn't stand the thought of anyone being hungry. It seemed to agree with her, and over the course of that sweltering summer, they fell into a routine that made life a bit easier.

Granddaddy liked his dinner ready when he walked in the door. During breakfast, Mamaw always asked where he'd be working that day so she could calculate dinnertime. She wanted everything to run smoothly.

Part of her routine was to visit with Dottie for a while each day. She would walk up the hill to her sister's house with her baby on her hip. After a cool glass of iced tea and some biscuits, she would be ready to face the garden and get dinner started.

Mamaw was developing her cooking skills, especially with vegetables. There was such abundance in her own yard, and waste was a sin. They shared their bounty with neighbors and the church. With the depression making things hard on everyone she was grateful to be able to help feed others in the community.

After two difficult pregnancies, the doctor advised them not to have another child. He even recommended a hysterectomy. The thought of that frightened her more than having another child. It had been 5 years since Betty was born.

Ruby and Betty were in Dottie's living room looking at dress patterns for Easter. Dottie had become quite a seamstress and loved making things for the girls. She needed to keep busy and not dwell on her own childless life.

Suddenly Mamaw burst in and told the girls to run home right away and take the wash off the line. They all looked at her curiously because she had such a frightened look on her face.

Ruby started to ask, "Mother what's …"

"Just do as you're told…NOW." She yelled.

They didn't often see her angry and agitated. Both ran out the door and down the hill.

Dottie looked at Mamaw and somehow knew what had her in such a state. Such a paradox, two sisters envious of each other's lot in life.

"How far along are you?" Dottie asked.

In early December Mamaw gave birth to a perfectly healthy boy. They named him James Ralph and called him by his middle name. She was amazed at how easily the time had flown with this pregnancy. Yet she didn't argue with her doctor when he suggested they ensure she wouldn't have another and swore him to secrecy. She felt six pregnancies in ten years with only four healthy living children was a sign.

With Betty in school, Mamaw could devote more time to the baby. Ruby, who was then ten, was quite capable of handling much of the housework and Charles could be helpful even though she didn't feel her two sons would have many common interests with an eight-year age difference.

Life was very routine in Mamaw's little world. She was content. She had her dear sister Dottie nearby and a strong church community around her. Some days she couldn't believe her good fortune.

A typical week began on Sunday, the Lord's Day, with church in the morning. Sometimes Grandaddy would preach, though he was only a Deacon. He wanted his own church one day, but their financial reality kept him in carpentry, and even that was becoming scarce. He traveled further outside of town than he liked, but you had to go where the work was.

Daddy duJour

They always went to Sunday and Wednesday evening Prayer Meetings, and he made sure the children were involved in Youth Group and Choir. Essentially church was the only life outside of home and school for his children. Over time this created some rebellion.

Five years passed quickly, and Ruby was becoming a young woman who resented having every moment of her life dictated. She began to find ways of circumventing the status quo which usually involved her younger sister covering for her. Betty didn't mind because she was rebellious by nature and not happy with all church all the time. They were in different stages of a search for forbidden fruit.

Mamaw was onto them. She heard the older church ladies buzzing about seeing Ruby with a boy on the other side of town and decided to do some detective work of her own.

Late one summer evening, when the girls were preparing to leave for choir practice, she decided to follow them. She dropped the boys at Dottie's house and went to church. She peered in the window of the parish hall and was relieved to see both girls. Maybe the old biddies were wrong, she thought?

She'd gotten the boys home and was putting Ralph to bed when she heard the front door. "I'm in here girls!" she hollered, certain neither suspected her of spying.

"It's just me, mother," Betty replied.

"Where's your sister?" Mamaw asked.

"Mr. Bradshaw asked her to stay and work on a song for Sunday," she replied.

Mamaw found nothing wrong with that. She knew Ruby had a beautiful voice and Granddaddy would be very proud if she had a solo at church next Sunday.

The three youngest were tucked in before Ruby came home. Mamaw was again suspicious.

"Why are you so late young lady?"

"Didn't Betty tell you Mr. Bradshaw asked me to stay and learn a song?" she asked.

"Two hours ago," Mamaw said. "That's an awfully long time, and it's late for a school night."

She noticed a flush to Ruby's cheeks and knew something had been going on besides singing. "I believe I'll have your father look into this with Mr. Bradshaw."

As Ruby turned to head for the bedroom, she said, "Oh mother! Don't be ridiculous! Why should daddy bother Mr. Bradshaw over a late choir practice?"

The bedroom door slammed sharply. Mamaw had to find a way to share her suspicions with Granddaddy without having him fly off the handle. She knew he would get to the bottom of it but also knew he ruled with a hickory switch.

Granddaddy would often line them up and give them the lecture, "This is going to hurt me more than it's going to hurt you..." before he started the beatings. Ruby was always the toughest. She could have blood running down her legs and never let him see a teardrop.

Mamaw was concerned about how this might play out. The next Sunday Grandaddy went to see Mr. Bradshaw after services.

Benton Bradshaw was a nice man about the same age as Mamaw. He'd moved to town the year before. He told everyone he had taught choir in a high school, but they changed the program and left him searching for work. He heard they needed a choir director in the church.

Granddaddy promised Mamaw he wouldn't even talk to Ruby about this incident until he spoke to Mr. Bradshaw first. Ruby wasn't sure what to expect when he came home. She was prepared for the worst and told Betty they would probably all get a beating and it was her fault.

Mamaw kept the Sunday meal warm waiting for Granddaddy. She too was afraid it would be an ugly afternoon with no one interested in food when he was finished. She was relieved to see Granddaddy was in a good mood.

Ruby sat at the table making eye contact with no one. She listened to her father recounting his conversation with Mr. Bradshaw while barely able to swallow a bite of food.

He told them what a good man Benton was and how he went on and on about Ruby's voice. "He wants her to have a solo every week, and he's going to work extra hard to help her do well. I think that's very nice of him Ruby and you better pay attention."

Mamaw knew it wasn't her voice Mr. Bradshaw was interested in.

Within that year Ruby became pregnant and married Benton. As she was starting her own family, Granddaddy took a job in Toledo, Ohio and moved the rest of his family north.

My mother met my father in Toledo at the Jeep plant where she worked part-time. Not long after they began dating, she became pregnant with me. She dropped out of school her sophomore year. My parents' relationship was rocky from the beginning, and by the time I was two they were divorced.

Chapter VII
Ross

I don't remember much about the second husband, Ross. I was three years old when they married.

He was mom's boss at the Jeep plant in Toledo. He knew my grandfather and used that relationship to come and hang out at their house while mom and I were living with them.

She wasn't the least bit interested in him, but he was very interested in her. Granddaddy thought he was a great guy and urged her to go out with him. He believed she needed a husband. It was the '50's after all.

Ross owned apartment buildings in addition to his supervisory position at the plant. All of that looked very upstanding to Granddaddy, but the more he pushed it on mom, the more she resisted.

Mom took a vacation week to go down to Georgia and visit family. We took a bus, I remember, and it was fun for me. There were a couple of soldiers on the bus, and whenever we stopped, they would get candy or soda for me.

Mom's sister, Ruby, picked us up at the bus station and drove us to her house, outside of Rome, GA. Ruby had a son, Benny, who was a year older than me. He had suffered from eye problems since the day he was born and had at least two surgeries by the time he was three.

Ruby and her husband, Benton, lived behind his gas station/ convenience store. He was quite a bit older than she and not a very nice man. Fortunately, he spent most of his time in the store.

A few days after we arrived Mamaw and Granddaddy showed up.

The next day Ross showed up. Mom was not happy. She knew it was Granddaddy's plan that brought Ross to Georgia. Her life was not her own.

I remember little about Ross and none of it good. He had blonde curly hair and a pale broad face with ice blue eyes. He never smiled, and always seemed uptight. He was of German and Polish descent and had a very cold nature.

I'm not sure if mom resisted because Granddaddy wanted her to like Ross or if she had some internal instinct about why she shouldn't.

After a week of family pow-wows, crying, yelling, and carrying on, Ross asked her to marry him. I can only imagine how overwhelming it must have been for mom. She was nineteen years old with a three-year-old child and had never been able to win an argument with her father no matter how hard she tried.

She finally gave in. They had a brief ceremony at my aunt's house with a justice of the peace. Shortly after he packed up the car, he was surprised to find out I was

Daddy duJour

going with them. I think he assumed I would go back with my grandparents, which would have been fine with me, but mom wanted me with her. I think she knew it would be a wedge between them.

We stopped at a motel somewhere in Kentucky, and they brought in a cot for me to sleep on. I had been used to sleeping with mom for a long time and didn't want to sleep alone.

She would tuck me in, and I would go get in bed next to her. She would put me back and…this went on a few times before Ross said, "I'll take care of her."

He proceeded to grab me by one arm and beat me as I dangled in the air in front of him.

Mom was screaming for him to stop and tried to pull me away. He shoved her down on the bed and continued until the noise brought a knock at the door.

The motel manager was there with the police. When all was said and done, Ross slept in the car.

I can only imagine what was going on in mom's mind, knowing how far we were from home and wondering what the hell Granddaddy had wrought. I'm sure he would never have expected this outcome but, here we were on her wedding night huddled together and scared to death.

We snuggled tight in the big bed but, I don't think we slept very much. I'm sure mom was trying to figure a way to quickly end this relationship after she saw how it was starting.

The next morning there was a knock at the door, and she looked outside. Ross was standing there with donuts and coffee and very politely asked her to let him in. She did.

He tried to apologize, even tried to hug me, but she stepped between. They talked for a while, and she agreed to drive back to Toledo with him. I doubt she had enough money with her to take the bus. The silence in the car was deafening.

By the time we arrived, he had told her they would be living in an apartment in one of his buildings and I would be living with my grandparents in a large apartment he'd arranged for them upstairs.

The building was in a decent part of town with old mansions that had been converted to apartment buildings. This was how Ross made his money. Most were three or four stories with at least two apartments per floor.

I have no idea what my grandfather thought of him after all of this, but they did agree to live there with me. Mom was able to quit her job, and we spent time together when Ross wasn't home.

One night, after I'd gone to bed, I heard them fighting. You couldn't miss it with all the yelling echoing in the hallway. I heard the front door slam and looked out the window. She was trying to run away but, he caught her and dragged her down the walk by her hair and beat her up against a telephone pole.

Daddy duJour

When granddaddy went outside to stop it, the cops showed up, and things settled down. I was only three but will never forget the scene. I can't recall if I screamed or stood silent. I only knew I didn't want to be anywhere near him.

Their marriage didn't last much more than a year, and I never lived with them. Whenever he would come to my grandparent's apartment, I would run to Granddaddy. I know Ross was abusive to her but, she seemed unable to leave. Perhaps my grandparents turned a blind eye to the continuing abuse or simply felt helpless to do anything about it.

It might have had something to do with the living arrangements. As I recall from conversations over the years, she left Ross shortly after my grandparents moved out of Ross' apartment building and into a new place. We stayed with them until she found her third husband, Al.

Chapter VIII

The Court Order

Spring had finally arrived in Waterville, and I hoped it would usher in a sunnier time for David and me. We didn't discuss the visit to Michigan after we left. We had gotten into a routine at Marvin and Lora's house. I liked the school there and enjoyed being a kid, some of the time. The next year would be Junior High, and I was ready for it.

I was a late bloomer. It could have been due to malnutrition earlier on, or not, but I finally needed a bra. By most anyone's standard, it would have been called a training bra, but I never understood where the training came in. I had been the adult in my family for a long time, so there was no more training needed, as far as I was concerned.

One Saturday afternoon Marvin invited me downstairs to show me something. You had to go outside and down the stone steps to get into the basement. I'd never been in there before. There had been no reason to.

It was a large space, filled mostly with boxes, and there was a kitchen table with a couple of chairs on either side of it. I saw a canoe in the back. I guess they used it on the river during the warm weather. It was rather dark and very damp in there.

Daddy duJour

"What do you want to show me?" I asked.

"Do you like cartoons and comic books?" he asked.

"Not really," I replied.

"You might like these," he said.

He handed me what looked like a comic book but, the cartoons were crude and pornographic. He stood very close to me as I flipped through it and I immediately felt the 'fight or flight' instinct. I threw the book at him and bolted for the door.

When I got upstairs and into my room, I couldn't stop shaking. "What the hell was that about?" I thought. But, immediately I knew, I needed a lock on my bedroom door. Should I tell Lora? Would she believe me? Did she know about it already? Something had to be done but what?

When she came to get me for dinner, I feigned being asleep. I couldn't sit at the table with Marvin after that incident. It would be better to try to sleep and figure everything out in the morning.

Later there was a knock on my door, and I jumped up, afraid it might be Marvin. It was Lora.

"Are you ok?" she asked.

"Yeah, I'm ok," I lied.

"There are leftovers if you get hungry," she said.

"What time is it?" I asked.

"It's about nine," she said.

"Could I get a lock on my door?" I asked.

"Why on earth would you need a lock on your door?" she asked.

"I just feel like I need some privacy and don't want the kids barging in," I lied.

She laughed but, the next day we went to the hardware store and got two locks. The bathroom door needed one, too.

On Memorial Day weekend, there was a big family cookout at Marvin and Lora's house. Al came with his other sister, Nancy, who lived in Akron, Ohio. The backyard was full of kids playing games and taking turns in the canoe. I slipped away upstairs to watch some TV in peace and quiet.

Suddenly a police car pulled up out front. I went to the window to see what was going on and that's when I saw my mother get out of a car behind it, and my grandmother was with her.

I ran out the door and down the stairs screaming, "My mom's here with the cops!!"

Then I grabbed David, ran into the basement and locked the door. David looked scared, which made sense, he only had to look at the panic on my face and feel the fear surging through my body to know something was terribly wrong.

Lora and Marvin went upstairs and left the kids out in the yard. They didn't seem too concerned about what was happening upstairs. I sat in the damp basement clinging to David and trembling.

Could she simply show up and take us away? Did anyone have a clue this was going to happen? Why was Mamaw with her? I wanted to throw up.

After a short while, Lora came down and asked me to unlock the door. She and Marvin came in and explained what was happening.

Mom had gotten a court order to get custody of us again. She swore we would have a decent home and responsible child care, which was the only way the court would allow this. That's the story I heard. I believed none of it.

It didn't matter what I believed. As a twelve-year-old, I had no say in any of it. She had a court order. Period.

As I walked up the outside stairs to the street level, she was standing at the top. I took one look and knew she was pregnant. She had gained weight and was wearing a loose shift dress. She reached for David as we got to the top and I pulled him toward me.

"You've kept my baby away from me long enough," she said.

"He's more mine than yours," I replied, "You didn't care about us when we were freezing in the trailer."

My grandmother stepped between us and said, "Jeanie, don't talk to your mother like that, she's been heartsick without you and the baby."

Barbara Hammond

Much of the family called me Jeanie, and I think the reason I preferred Barb or Barbara was because it separated me from them, somehow.

"Mamaw, you don't know what she's done and if you did you wouldn't let her take us," I said.

The officer stepped in and suggested everyone go inside and calm down. We went inside, and while the adults looked over the court order and resigned themselves to what was, I was packing up our belongings and wondering what would happen next.

There was no way out of this. It was so defeating. As much as I loved my grandmother I had a very difficult time understanding how she could condone this. She and Granddaddy had been involved in some of the court drama. They knew what was going on but, in the end, they stood with their daughter, right or wrong. It really hurt.

On that awful Memorial Day, as we drove out of Waterville, I got part of mom's story on the way to my grandparents' house. She went on about how painful this had been for her, which was the norm with mom. Never concerned for her kids, but always the martyr.

When we arrived at my grandparents' home, they started unloading the car.

"We're living with Mamaw and Granddaddy?" I asked.

"You'll be staying here for a while," she said, "I found a small apartment close to work."

Daddy duJour

I looked at Mamaw hoping for some insight, and she avoided eye contact. Something was fishy, and I couldn't put my finger on it.

To get the court order allowing her to take us she had to prove she had a safe place for us to live with her. She lied because she wasn't living there. She had gotten a one-room apartment close to the dive bar where she worked. Not the nicest area of town. So typical of her.

The first few days went by with her coming to visit during the day acting all gaga over her baby boy and giving me wide berth. Then one day, she announced her landlady, whom none of us had ever met, had agreed to babysit while she was working. There was one little hitch though; the apartment was only big enough for her to add a crib for David so I would be staying with my grandparents.

My gut told me this was not a good idea, but I was powerless to stop her from leaving with David. I remember my grandmother saying, "Now you know how much your mother loves you. She's changed now, and you have to accept it." I believed neither comment.

My uncle Ralph, who's only eleven years older than me, was like my big brother. He and his wife, Jean, were always there for us when we needed them, providing they knew where we were.

Ralph had polio when he was a child and wore a brace on one leg. It had limited the work he could sometimes do, but he'd found a good job at a plumbing and heating company, mostly driving their truck.

His wife, Jean, was a gift in our lives. She was a large woman with a larger heart. There were so many times I had stayed with them over the years. Their first child was two months older than David and twice his size.

They lived about a mile from my grandparents. I wanted to talk to them about this new development, so I walked over to their house, the day after mom left with David.

We were all in agreement, Ralph, Jean, and me, about not being able to trust mom, so he suggested he should go to mom's new apartment while she was working, so he could see how the new babysitter was working out. I made him take me. It was worse than we even anticipated.

The area had been a very wealthy neighborhood many years before. Large stately homes had become run down rooming houses over the years. If you squinted, you could see the former majesty. Wide stone steps leading to a double door that was, no doubt, mahogany under multiple layers of chipped paint. Inside a foyer with what once had a grand staircase now had cheap paneling and multiple doors along the hallway. We knocked on the door with 'MGR' on it.

A disheveled old lady opened the door. She was clearly drunk. I was cursing my gut for being right. My uncle asked if she was babysitting his nephew. She looked at him quizzically before it dawned on her sotted brain what he was referring to.

Daddy duJour

"Oh, sure! Sweet kid. Sleeps all the time." She said. We pushed our way in, and she said, "Oh, he's not here. He's in his own crib. He likes it there."

I thought my uncle was going to choke her, but he stopped himself. He knew it wasn't this old lady he wanted to choke; it was his sister. I thought he had better get to her before I did!

She took us down the hall to mom's disgusting apartment. I heard him crying before she opened the door. Then I began to cry. His crib was next to the double bed which took up the majority of the room. There was a small bathroom on the left, and behind the wall, the bed was against, was a tiny kitchenette. The shades were drawn, and no light was on.

He was standing in his crib with a filthy diaper dragging down past his knees that most likely hadn't been changed since morning. His little face was red and swollen from crying for God knows how long. He reached up to me, and I just crumpled.

How the hell could ANYone do this to an innocent child? How could ANY court system give this person custody?! My tears turned to rage. I wanted to kill her. I saw the same look in my uncle's eyes. We just stared at each other for a moment then he said, "Grab the baby and let's go."

We figured out our plan on the way to his house.

Ralph contacted Al, and everything was set in motion. We couldn't tell Mamaw and Granddaddy what we were going to do, but they were very upset to learn about the conditions she had left David in. They had trusted mom and, once again, she let everyone down.

When mom called Mamaw, she knew what had happened. She knew we took David and I'm sure she knew why. She cried and apologized but, Mamaw told her it was best if David and I stayed with them. Mom kept silent.

A few days after we brought David back from the dump she left him in I told Mamaw I was taking him for a walk. She had kept a stroller at their house, and I crammed as much as I could get into the diaper bag and the bottom rack of the stroller.

We walked over to Ralph's house and waited for Al to pick us up. He drove us back to Waterville, but not to Lora's house. Everyone knew mom would go there first. Instead, we went to the sheriff's house. Al had done some handy work for him when we lived in Waterville, and they became friends. He was happy to help.

I knew Sharon, the sheriff's daughter, from school. She was very sweet and sympathetic to our situation. Everyone was prepared for a huge fight, but it was fairly quiet the first couple of days. I didn't go to school for fear she would look for me there, and Sharon brought books home from school for me, which occupied my time.

A week went by and, as far as I knew, nothing had happened. There were court dates I heard them talking about, but no one gave me details. When the sheriff

Daddy duJour

came home and told me Al and my mother were getting back together, I was dumbfounded.

This would be their third try at making their marriage work. Even though they were divorced, or so I thought, he still loved her, and she needed him for many reasons.

He knew about the baby and willingly agreed to claim it as his own. It was awkward for me, because I knew better, but admired him for being such a good guy.

Al bought a small brick house that was brand new. It was the nicest place we'd ever lived, even if the neighborhood was a bit iffy. There were three bedrooms and a big kitchen. I had a room of my own and David would share one with the baby when it came.

I started 7th grade in a new school, but nothing could have been harder than changing schools four times in 6th grade, even though I went to one school twice that year. I was ready for stability.

Chapter IX

New Beginnings?

We moved into the new house full of hope. Over the summer, mom embraced the role of homemaker, which surprised everyone. New furniture was delivered, and she was even cooking. All seemed right with the world.

Mom had stopped working as soon as they took possession of the house, and she loved her new role as matriarch. The baby was due in September. Everyone seemed happy and satisfied.

She enrolled me in a modeling school that began in September. It was evening classes and a lot of fun. I was short, 5'2", and definitely skinny, which was the new trend in the early '60's. It was the first activity I felt was my own. I was not tending to another soul. It was freeing, for sure.

The modeling school, Patricia Stevens, was a chain. They weren't grooming the next cover of Vogue, by any stretch of the imagination. But, the only thing I knew about style and fashion was what I saw on TV.

My mother usually looked like the painted lady. She was short and cute but, often went overboard on make-up, I thought. She didn't have any fashion sense. Everything she wore was tight and short, and she bleached her hair to the point of straw.

Daddy duJour

When I began learning how to apply make-up in class, my mother disagreed with their way of doing it. I never wore more than pink lipstick to school but, they were teaching me how to shape my eyebrows and apply mascara. At thirteen years old, I felt that was about all I really needed.

But, mom couldn't wait to show me her version when I came home from classes. It was a clown school, in my opinion. When I expressed my feelings, she would throw something and storm out of my room. I would see girls in the restrooms at school applying lots of make-up in the mornings and it kind of made me laugh. If I had left for school the way mom would have preferred, I would have been washing my face before class.

The baby was born September 29, 1963, by cesarean section, as her previous deliveries had been. She had little difficulty and seemed to revel in caring for her new son, Tim. Al was a proud papa. Only a few people knew he wasn't the biological father and that was a positive.

David loved being the big brother. The family dynamic was changing for the better, with everyone fulfilling their own roles.

Al was laid off from the factory again, shortly after the New Year. Being together, 24/7 wasn't working very well for mom, and she decided to pick up a bartending gig for extra cash. Al wasn't happy about it at all, but couldn't argue they needed the money.

The only work Al had ever had was factory work. I don't know for sure what his skillset was but, he was very handy with cars and odd jobs around the house.

He filled his time painting the bedrooms and other projects and, reading trashy paperbacks. It wasn't long before they were back to fighting regularly. He was jealous, by nature, and often would go sit at her bar at night. They'd come home late, arguing and shouting at each other.

While Al was painting their bedroom, fire engine red, he asked me to come and keep him company. I didn't think anything of it. He had a radio on and was cracking jokes for a while, then got very serious. I was sitting at the foot of the bed, and he sat down beside me.

"You know, I don't know why I'm painting this room red," he said. "Your mother isn't looking for passion in here, that's for sure. She's frigid," he said. "Do you know what that means?"

I didn't have a clue, so he proceeded to explain. It was awkward and made me very uncomfortable. This was a man who had been my father, in the true sense of that relationship, for eight years. Now he was telling me about their sex life? Or lack of sex life?

He put his hand on my knee, and I froze. What the hell was going on?

"I really have to get my homework done," I said, as I bolted out the door and into my room.

A few nights later he walked in on me in the bathroom. I was in the tub and immediately recoiled and asked him to leave. He did. Later that night he made a comment about pubic hair and my going through puberty. I retreated to my room and locked the door.

I wasn't sure what might happen if I told mom, so I didn't. If she knew, I would become fodder for her leaving and that would have made things worse. As it turned out, she was very close to making a move anyway.

The next night Al started talking about one of the books he was reading.

"This guy is sleeping with his daughter. Can you believe it?" he asked no one in particular.

Mom told him to stop reading trash, and he interrupted her with, "I could see it if it was a step-daughter...."

I froze. Mom looked at me like she was wondering if something was going on between Al and me. Then she saw my face and knew better.

The next morning she was packing some of our things, and she took us out to my grandparents for the weekend. While we were at Mamaw and Granddaddy's, she went back to pack up the rest of our things. It was kind of her to remove us from the middle of an ugly fight but, left me with no idea where we'd end up. The school year was almost over, and I couldn't even guess where I'd be going for ninth grade.

It was during the move I learned mom hadn't remarried Al, so it was a clean break. Who needed the drama of another divorce? Most of them had been uncontested anyway, with very little drama on the surface, but with mom, there was always drama.

She found a duplex in a new school district and, the school was easy walking distance. There was an older woman, Mrs. Welker, living downstairs with her grown son and she was thrilled to have children in the house.

The boys would stay in her apartment while I was in school and mom at work. I would bring them upstairs when I got home. Often Mrs. Welker would give me casseroles to heat for dinner. They were always good and always welcome.

This was a huge step up from the trailer. I was grateful for that but, really sick of being the new kid. I didn't even attempt to make friends in the new school. It was enormous. It took me forever, it seemed, to learn the routes from one class to another.

One day a cute boy came to my locker at the end of the day and asked if he could walk me home.

"We go in the same direction, so I thought we could walk together," he said. It wasn't like being asked on a date but, it made sense. I agreed.

Peter was a junior and, obviously, taking different classes than I had so we didn't have a lot of school-related topics to talk about. He told me about trying out for the basketball team but not making it. It didn't really

Daddy duJour

bother him, he said. His dad wanted him to try out, but Peter's heart wasn't in it.

I had never had time to get involved in any after-school activities. Mine were home waiting for me every day. Peter and I were more bookish than athletic, for sure. So we talked about books and classes we enjoyed like English and History, not much else.

One day I invited him in but, he said he had to get home. He did walk me to the door, though, and kissed me. I was taken off guard but didn't mind. It was my first kiss.

The stairway up to our apartment was inside, and after he broke the ice with the first kiss, we would spend time inside on the steps making out for a while. He always kept an eye on the time so he could get home before his dad.

Having a warm place to live and knowing neighbors were close and caring, made this time less stressful. It was a decent part of town, no drunken neighbors or creepy streets to walk through.

One night mom came home earlier than expected and I heard her talking to someone at the bottom of the stairs. I tried to eavesdrop and knew it was a man. It sounded very cozy, so I opened the door and looked downstairs.

They both looked up at me, and mom said, "That's my nosy daughter. Get back inside."

I closed the door, and a few minutes later she came up. I expected her to be giving me grief for checking out the guy, but she didn't.

"Isn't he handsome?" she asked.

"He looked like every other bum you've ever brought home," I said.

"Why do you have to be such a bitch?" she asked.

I didn't dare respond. She didn't want to know what was going through my mind, so I simply walked away.

I was five when Al came into our lives and thirteen when he was banished. I had seen my mother taunt him with her behavior and cheating over the years and watched him keep coming back for more.

She was never long without a man in her life because she was always searching for the love she'd never felt she received from her father. At the ripe old age of thirty mom was looking for her fourth husband.

Chapter

X

Les

It was the fourth husband, who verified my instincts about people. I had him pegged the moment I laid eyes on him in the stairwell.

His name was Les. He worked for the Toledo Blade newspaper as a typesetter. Not a rich man but, financially comfortable. She was gaga for this guy.

She was insulted when I called him a bum. According to her, he was so smart, so sweet and nice and, he had a great job, yadda yadda yadda. My gut said otherwise. There was something about his icy blue eyes and sideways smirk that whispered trouble.

We had just moved into our apartment, in a decent area of town, shortly before Les came into the picture. I had started 9th grade at a new high school. In nine years this was the twelfth school I'd attended. Having a broad frame of reference, I felt it was a pretty good school.

Mom was working nights which meant I had to rush home from school. Mrs. Welker had the boys for a couple of hours but couldn't keep them past 3 or 4 pm. No after-school activities for me, but I was used to that.

Within weeks Les was around a lot. He had clearly been anointed the next in succession. I could not warm up to this guy at all but knew I was doomed to this fate.

We moved to a larger apartment around Christmas time. Les had been spending most of his time with us, so we needed more space. I would have preferred separate States, but any extra space was welcome, and it was in the same school district.

Les was very attentive to the baby, Tim, but barely tolerant of the four-year-old, David. As for me, I believe we had a mutual distrust that grew over time. Keeping that in mind, you can only imagine how I took the news, in early February, that they were getting married. Seems 'Mother of the Century' was pregnant!

They chose Valentine's Day for a civil ceremony early in the morning. Afterward Les went to work and later that day so did mom. It was just another Friday, or so it seemed.

Les never came home. Imagine the bride's shock when she arrived back at the apartment at 2:15 am to find her brand new hubby had never returned from work! She woke me in a panic.

"Why didn't you call to tell me he hadn't come home?" she screamed.

"I didn't realize I was babysitting your husband," I replied as I pulled the covers over my head, hoping he had changed his mind and left town for good.

Daddy duJour

In her total hysteria, she called one of his friends from work. His friend had no idea where he could be and wasn't even aware they had gotten married. She called a couple of other people, too but, no one seemed to know anything. She called the police... no accidents reported. He wasn't in any hospital in town. He was just gone.

She called in sick on Saturday and frequently checked in with his friends hoping they'd heard from him. Nothing.

I wanted to say to her, "I told you he was a worthless bum!" But, she was so pathetic I couldn't. I felt sorry for her. I had never seen her so distraught she was almost panic-stricken. I'm sure the pregnancy played into the emotional aspect. I tried to keep my distance and keep the kids out of her way.

Around 3pm Sunday afternoon Les came waltzing in the door. We were frozen in anticipation. He seemed jovial and confused as to why she was so upset. But, when she mentioned she'd spoken to his friends and co-worker's things got very scary.

He grabbed her by her hair virtually lifting her off the floor, pulling her head back to face him, and hissed through clenched teeth, "If you EVER do anything like that again you will live to regret it! Do you understand me?!"

She tried to explain her fear that something had happened to him and he cut her off. "My comings and goings are none of your goddamned business!"

And the games began.

Les was 5'10" and maybe 140lb. His pompadour added a couple of inches to his height. He literally was so skinny when he crossed his legs he could wrap his ankle around the back of his other leg. When he was angry, his pompadour shook a little.

Despite his wiry physique, he had an air of evil about him. Those icy blue eyes, which were rarely smiling, seemed almost demented, to me. I never trusted him, and he'd gone a long way toward making mom afraid of him. We all were.

Shortly after he set the rules straight, according to his view, he announced he'd found a nice house with more room and we would be moving the next week! No discussion, no concern about changing schools mid-year, it was done. I was relieved to learn it was a good school district since this would be my thirteenth school in nine years.

It was a ranch house in a typical suburban neighborhood with a large backyard for the kids. We were hopeful. Les had been well-behaved, and mom had quit her job after learning she was pregnant. She totally immersed herself in becoming a housewife. This was comforting but, I was always waiting for the other shoe to drop.

As odd as living with Les was, things started to seem normal. At least as normal as they ever could be. He had a good job, which eliminated the money stress, and mom was actually staying home with her little ones and letting me out of the house once in a while to be with friends.

The illusion of calm made it easier to adapt to his moods when he came home from work. If he was whistling as he walked in the door, we exhaled, if not, we braced ourselves. He was occasionally MIA, but we never discussed it. It was just like the '50's TV show, 'Father Knows Best'! HA!

One afternoon as I walked in the door after school there was a quiet discussion going on at the kitchen table. It seemed very serious but not heated. A little while later we were having a family powwow.

Les had two sons with his first wife. This was news to me and, apparently to mom. The youngest was in a home, of some sort, in Georgia. The older boy was coming to live with us. He was ten years old, and the ex-wife threatened to put him in a home if Les didn't take him. Nice. She sounded like a perfect match for Les, which is most likely why he left her. The step-brother arrived within a week.

Things were awkward for a while. Everyone was making a concerted effort to be nice to one another, even Les for a while. He'd had no lasting relationship with his son before so it was like taking in a border, really.

Over the summer my brother, David, was diagnosed with a double hernia. He was only four, but the doctor felt he would sail right through it. The surgery was scheduled for mid-July.

This was 1964, and any surgery was, on average, a three to five-day stay. David's surgery was Tuesday morning. On Tuesday afternoon my mother was rushed to a different hospital due to vaginal bleeding. They had to deliver the baby and hope for the best. She'd had three cesarean births, and with this one, the uterine scar was rupturing.

He was three months premature, weighed 3lb. 2oz. and lived less than 48hrs. Today that would be considered a robust preemie, and I'm sure he would have survived. God truly works in mysterious ways.

The logistics of that week were mind-boggling. David admitted Monday, surgery Tuesday morning. Mom's emergency C-section Tuesday afternoon, the baby died early Thursday. David released Friday, baby's funeral Saturday, mom home Monday.

I didn't visit mom and never saw the baby. Not because I didn't want to but because it wasn't logistically possible. I felt sorry for her and sad about the loss. None of us knew how she would handle it. My grandparents, aunt and uncle, and I had been in a rotation staying at the hospital with my brother or, taking care of the other two boys.

Unlike any other times in my life, mom was desperately trying to be a good wife and mother. This was foreign to her, and I appreciated her effort. She had made attempts with Al but, this was different. She was learning how to cook, and she baked a cake every Friday night. Les loved chocolate cake, and she wanted him

Chapter

XI

Siblings

I was still adjusting to a stepbrother who was physically my size but four years younger. He was a nice enough kid but, he came with as much baggage as I had. Leaving a brother who had developmental problems that I still don't know about, and moving in with a father he barely knew, plus a step-mother and siblings, it had to be overwhelming.

The night came when we had an ugly incident, and things got physical.

We had been blithely going through our day to day ignoring the elephant in the room. I was trying to ignore everyone, deal with school and enjoy my respite from responsibility. Step-brother was walking around with a huge chip on his shoulder trying to figure out how to fit in.

One Friday night mom and Les were going out and leaving me to babysit. It had been quite a while since the summer ugliness, and I honestly felt mom deserved a night out.

I settled in to watch TV and step-brother walked in and changed the channel. The gauntlet was thrown. Me, at 5'2" and weighing about 90lb. soaking wet, and he was

Daddy duJour

a bit shorter but beefy. I told him to change it back, and he said, "Make me."

Somehow in the back of my head, I had anticipated this for months. We weren't close. In fact, I don't believe we ever had an honest one on one discussion about anything since he'd arrived.

The craziness that was July had been swept under the rug, and all of us had unresolved issues. We were living a lie, as opposed to living the dream, so to speak.

With all the pent-up anxiety, it didn't take long for this to turn very ugly. He punched me, and it was on. I went to my room, got the heaviest belt I owned, and proceeded to show him who was in charge. I'm not proud of it, but boundaries had to be established.

To my amazement, he never said a word to anyone. Somehow in a heated, physical battle between two kids trying to make sense of the insanity they were living in came understanding, even a bond. It was as if we had taken out all our frustrations on each other and came to mutual respect. In a way, we became allies in our strange world.

Shortly after school started, my junior year in high school, Les threw us another curve. Just as he had taken it upon himself to announce our move to the house we were in, he decided to take it a step further.

In the middle of dinner on a night he had come in whistling, a night we were relaxed, defenses down, he announced he'd bought a house in Michigan. We were moving to another state.

No one was more surprised than my mother. She asked, "Why? We're all very happy here."

"It was time to buy a house, and you will all be happy in it." He said. Then got up, left the table and all the gaping mouths behind him.

The next day he came home in a new station wagon. Apparently, he intended to become a true suburbanite. He took my mother up to see the new house, leaving the rest of us to wonder. She came home very excited.

"Barb, I am telling you this is the nicest house you've ever seen!" she said.

"It's just across the state line, so we won't be far from everyone, but it's like another world, to me."

Somehow I knew the physical house couldn't make the fractured souls who would be living in it, whole. Like lipstick on a pig, as they say. Within weeks we were crossing the state line and moving this train wreck.

It was, in fact, a brand new, contemporary ranch house. It had a cathedral ceiling in the living room, large eat-in kitchen, one full and one half-bath with a new washer and dryer in it. There were three bedrooms on one side of the house. I had the front corner bedroom between the older boys' room and the master bedroom. There was a small study on the other side of the house they turned into a bedroom for my baby brother, Tim, who was almost two when we moved in.

Daddy duJour

Mom was in her glory! You've never seen a more devoted domestic diva in your life. She had a big kitchen to cook and bake in, she was washing and ironing daily, she started gardening, too. It was overkill.

Everyone settled into their respective schools. Life seemed calm. We had lived with the psychological abuse for over a year, but the only physical abuse had been on his return from the honeymoon for one so, I think, we were lulled into a false sense of security.

One evening, as we sat having dinner together, Les seemed stranger than usual. He hadn't come in whistling. He never seemed normal to me, but this was different. Then step-brother reached for a second pork chop, and all hell broke loose.

Les jumped up, grabbed the kid by his shirt and slammed him into the wall. When he crumpled to the floor, Les kicked him then dragged him into his bedroom and continued beating him. We had no idea what the hell brought it on, nor did we dare to interfere.

My little brother, David, was clinging to the back of his chair looking completely terrified, which we all were. I disliked Les and never trusted him before that day but hadn't physically feared him. Now the fear in that house was so palpable you had to force your way through it.

Shortly after we had moved on in silence, yet again, we were preparing for the new school year, shopping for clothes and supplies, etc., and I was looking forward to my senior year.

Barbara Hammond

A few weeks before school started Les pulled another disappearing act. He worked for the newspaper, in their printing plant, and the union went on strike. There had been a lot of discussions between mom and Les about the what-ifs prior to the strike.

He mentioned several of the guys at work were going to take positions in St. Louis or Cincinnati if they could get in. He never mentioned he was thinking about leaving for work elsewhere. He just left.

After a week, with no word from Les, mom was getting very nervous about the finances. She went to the bank and discovered he had pulled out every last dime they had.

We were in full crisis mode now. My grandparents came to stay for a while, helping with groceries, kids and keeping mom calm. Granddaddy took mom to the welfare office to see if we could get aid for dependent children and food stamps. It was the first time she'd ever had to do such a thing. She was humiliated and beaten down by the entire process. I felt sorry for her.

School had begun, and Les was still gone. Mom had to go back to work. The only thing she really knew how to do was tend bar. She found a truck stop on the state line that hired her. I was babysitting again. We managed.

A few weeks after mom started her job Les came back. No warning, no fanfare, no explanation. I came home from school, and there he was, holding mom's hand with tears in his eyes. I wanted to throw up.

Daddy duJour

They both looked like they'd been crying. The newspaper strike had ended, and he was back at his old job. I knew she wanted things to work out but, she could never trust him again.

She insisted she was going to keep her job and he wasn't thrilled about that. She was challenging his control. I knew this was going to be trouble.

A few nights later I woke up to a loud banging and mom screaming. I ran out of my room and saw him beating her head against their closet door. I immediately ran to the kitchen to call the police. I didn't have a chance to dial before he came up and grabbed the receiver from me and punched me in the stomach with it.

Mom came running in yelling at him and the next thing I knew we were both up against the wall, and he was beating the crap out of us. I remembered someone telling me once if a man attacks you knee him in the groin. That was impossible because he was dancing around us like Muhammad Ali in the ring and we were trapped.

Then, as if someone turned a switch, he stopped and walked out of the kitchen. I looked at mom. Her face was a mess. She was bleeding from her mouth and had at least one black eye. I led her to a stool at the kitchen counter.

As I stood on the opposite side of the counter looking at her, I opened a drawer and saw the meat tenderizer (a metal hammer like utensil with sharp teeth on one side). I seriously considered pulling it out and whacking him over the head with it. Then a thought ran through my head, 'what if you miss?' He would have killed me with it, I'm sure.

As I was having these thoughts, he came back into the kitchen and began making coffee as if nothing had happened.

I said, "Come on mom, let's get out of here."

He said, "Yeah, you better get out of here." And out of my smart-ass mouth, as I reached down to retrieve a shred from my nightgown, came "Right!"

He was right on my heels, and when I reached my room, he spun me around and punched me square in the nose. Blood was spurting out all over me, and I was sure he had broken it. He turned around and walked away.

Mom and I sat there looking at each other, completely in shock. She got a T-shirt out of a drawer for me to hold over my nose to stop the bleeding while we were trying to figure out what to do next. He walked back in and said to her, "I think you'd better come to bed now."

"I can't leave her like this." She said.

"She'll live." He said.

I told her to go because I knew it would only get worse if she didn't.

I snuck into the boys' room and found them huddled together in one bed scared out of their minds. I tried to assure them we would be fine but I hadn't looked at myself in the mirror yet. When I did, it was obvious my appearance hadn't reassured them at all!

Les was the only one who slept that night. Bright and early in the morning he got up showered, had his coffee, read the paper, and left for work as if nothing had happened. As soon as he was gone, I called my uncle, Ralph, who came immediately and took us to the hospital first and police station second. Aunt Jean stayed at our house with the boys who were too shaken to go to school.

Mom had a broken jaw. They wired it back together and patched her up. My nose, thank God, wasn't broken but they were concerned about internal bruising in my abdomen. We were given medication and left.

The trip to the police station was much less helpful. We spoke to a very nice policeman who displayed as much sympathy as he could muster but ultimately couldn't do anything. We learned our new state had a 48 hour waiting period for domestic abuse cases.

"In case the 'little lady' changes her mind"! We went home, packed some things and moved in with my Uncle Ralph and Aunt Jean until we could figure out what to do next.

Chapter XII

The End of Les

The worst was over. Mom told me she had filed the police report after the cooling off period. I felt safe at Ralph and Jean's home. Getting to school was a challenge but, Step-brother and I only missed a few days.

A couple of weeks went by, and mom drove up to my uncle's house in the station wagon. Les' station wagon. My heart sank.

She told me she was going to get groceries. Instead, she was lured into a bullshit rendezvous with Les. No doubt, he seemed humble with his pleading. "I'm so sorry baby... I swear I will never hurt you again baby... Please take me back and let me prove it to you."

Sadly, this is so typical in domestic abuse cases. You can free your body long before you can free your mind from an abusive relationship. The mind keeps reeling you back in. You don't want to believe he was, perhaps, trying to kill you. No one ever wants to believe anything so heinous about someone they want to believe loves them.

I freaked out. I told her I wasn't going back and I wouldn't let her take the kids. It was quickly pointed out to me that I had no right to prevent her from taking the kids.

There was no way I could let her take them into that situation alone. I felt I had to go to protect them. I was delusional, obviously.

Uncle Ralph drove back with us. He had a message for Les, and it was actually fun to watch. My uncle was a big guy. As Les sat in a kitchen chair with his skinny legs twisted in a knot and his pompadour shaking, the conversation went something like this:

"You want a fight?"

"No, sir."

"Of course you don't want to fight a man, you cowardly son of a bitch, you prefer to beat up on women and children!"

"No, sir I don't."

"But you did."

"I lost my mind, and I apologized and will never lay a hand..."

"If you EVER even think about touching anyone in this house again I will personally come here and beat you within an inch of your miserable life."

"I swear..."

"Do you understand me?!"

"Yes, sir."

As with most reconciliation, there is a very short honeymoon period. Within a week the head games were starting all over again. I alerted Uncle Ralph.

With some outside help from a friend of moms, we were able to convince her she was living with a ticking time bomb. We finally made a move back to Ralph and Jean's house, for a while.

I have no degree in psychology, but life has made me an expert on Battered Woman Syndrome. Ironically that term didn't even exist in the '60's.

Research shows that violence begets violence. I'm certain my grandfather was beaten as a child and raised with the mantra 'spare the rod, spoil the child.' He, in turn, carried that tradition forward. He never laid a hand on my grandmother, but the kids got severe beatings.

As a female child, being beaten by her father, mom believed it was ok to beat your kids. She also believed if you were being mistreated by a man, it must be your fault.

Here are the four stages of BWS:

1) Denial. Making excuses for the abuser's behavior.

2) Guilt. The victims blame themselves and make excuses for themselves. For example, I'm not trying hard enough to understand him, to please him, maybe if I try harder, etc.

3) Enlightenment. The light bulb begins to flicker, and you recognize it's his fault but hope he'll change.

happy. It seemed unfair that she lost the baby, but I do believe it was a blessing for the baby.

The day she came home Les announced, "We are not going to talk about this... ever." That's easier said than done when you have other children trying to understand what happened. I told them the baby had gone to Heaven and we didn't want to upset mom by asking a lot of questions. They never mentioned it in front of her. But, I had them individually and collectively in my room looking for answers, at times. I simply couldn't find any.

A month later I came home from a date to find mom sitting in the middle of the living room floor surrounded by photographs. She was sobbing uncontrollably, and I immediately went to her. She just swept her arms out at the array of photographs all over the floor and looked at me like a wounded animal. They were photos of the baby and the funeral.

Apparently, they had gotten into an argument, and as he was walking out the door, he threw the pictures at her. I was stunned. What kind of evil son of a bitch does something like that? He didn't come home for three days.

With all the raw emotions, everyone was left with after the baby's death none were ever dealt with. After a while, things seemed to be back to our cracked normal and life went on.

4) Responsibility. Begin to take steps to leave. Realize only he can fix himself.

Battered Woman Syndrome is a form of Post-Traumatic Stress Disorder. I'm sure it's because living in a violent home feels like living in a war zone.

It astounds me how our society and the laws governing our society look at this type of violence differently than someone beaten up in a bar fight.

On any given night in our fair city, or yours, a woman is beaten within a breath of her life by her significant other and then left with the onus of proving it.

We, here in the U.S., have no solid national laws governing domestic violence so I feel we must all take a good hard look at this and bring the ugliness into the light.

One more thing,

Men aren't always the abusers. I want to share this story with you.

Scott's story:

My step-father, Al, went to great lengths to make my mother happy after he agreed to take her back and pretend her illegitimate child was his. He bought her the brand new house, for starters.

It was in a rundown neighborhood attempting to generate new life by building small ranch homes. They were identical inside but in different shades of brick outside. It was a giant leap from the trailer my mother had been living in.

I had my own room for the first time in my life, and for décor, I was given carte blanche. I painted it lavender and found pink and lavender striped curtains with a bedspread to match. It made me happy.

Shortly after we settled in, new neighbors moved into the red brick house next door. They had a son, Scott, who was ten years old. The mother, Roslyn, was at least six feet tall, which seemed funny to me because the father, Hank, was maybe five feet four. It didn't take long to see who ruled their roost.

At first, things seemed normal. Normal being a relative term, based on my life experience to this point. They argued loudly, but the same noise was wafting down the street from our house half the time, too.

The difference was how alcohol fueled their fights to a level I'd never seen. It usually occurred on weekends, but not always.

I would see Scott waiting for the school bus in the morning, yawning and rubbing his eyes. I knew they were dragging him out of bed late at night to watch them fight. I could hear it all from my bedroom window.

"Sit down kid! Watch me teach your daddy a lesson!"

Then she would start beating on her husband and laughing like a hyena. She must have known how to ensure no bruises would show because he never had a black eye or any outward signs of abuse I could see.

Their poor son was another story. He had the look and demeanor of an abused man, himself. The dark circles under his eyes and the saddest face you could imagine on a sweet little boy broke my heart.

One morning, after a very late and loud night, I told him, "If you want to sneak out, you can knock on my window, and I'll let you in."

"But, she would just come looking for me, and you'd get in trouble," he said.

"Do you think she could figure it out when she is so drunk?" I asked.

A few nights later I heard tapping on the window. I helped him in quickly, and we sat on the floor listening for what might happen next.

"SCOTTY!" she screamed.

We could hear her banging on the door to his room, which was the mirror image of mine, about twelve feet away.

"Open this fucking door, you little brat! Get your ass out here NOW!"

"I moved my dresser in front of the door," he whispered.

It was quiet for a moment before the beating began again. Apparently, she was more focused on beating her husband than torturing her son.

This became routine for Scott and me, at least once a week.

Christmas week was the turning point. It began when Scott's dad went out with a friend to cut down their Christmas tree.

It was just getting dark when I heard them coming up the street. Carols were blasting from the radio, windows down with evergreen sticking out of each one. Clearly, they had been drinking.

I had to laugh, as I watched two inebriated men wrestling with what looked like a bush. Somehow they managed to get it into the house. My imagination ran wild, wondering where they would place this tree that looked like a huge shrub.

Roslyn came home from work, and the games began. It was low, like a rumble, at first, but in a short time, it was full on.

"What are you, some kind of fucking idiot? That's not a Christmas tree!!"

Try as he might, Hank couldn't get a word in. Her rant was building to such a crescendo I thought she would burst a vein. Then I saw her drag Scott into the living room.

My parents weren't home, at the time, and I was tempted to call the cops but worried that might make things worse. All I could do was watch the shadows in the window and hope Scott could escape.

As the night wore on Hank began to sober up, but Roslyn was just getting juiced up. Suddenly it got very quiet.

"What the fuck do you think you're doing?!" she yelled.

I heard the side door open and saw her pinning Scott against the wall. He had the phone in his hand.

"Who you callin' ? The cops? HUH??" She screamed.

"No!" he lied.

"Who were you calling?" She demanded.

That's when Hank came up behind her and shoved her out the door. It was full on brawl right under my window. I called the cops.

When they arrived, she was beating Hank over the head with the phone. There was no denying who the victim was, as far as the cops were concerned. But, I knew who the true victim was.

Scotty was placed in child services, and I never saw him again. I used to imagine he found a wonderful, loving, foster family who appreciated what a sweet boy he was. I still hang onto that thought.

This is my grandparents at their 50th.

Me at 3

Scotty walking me down the aisle

The Wedding

The Reception

Packing for the honeymoon.

Packing the car for the honeymoon.

Scotty and I in the '80's.

Our 50th anniversary

Part II

Chapter XIII

Transitioning

Whenever I share any of these childhood stories with others I'm asked, "How did you turn out normal?"

I usually respond, "Normal is a relative term."

We all have our personal 'normal,' don't we? It's what we've come to expect. How things happened in our lives, regularly. Not always good, but somehow expected.

The other reason I like to feel I came out, somewhat normal, is because of my grandparents and my Aunt Jean and Uncle Ralph, during the tough years.

I know my grandfather was physically abusive to his children. I've heard enough stories over the years to believe it. But, he never laid a hand on me.

I remember one time when we were living with Al, and I was about eight, we were visiting my grandparents, and I made some smart alec remark about something Granddaddy had said. I can't remember what it was but, as soon as I said it and Granddaddy didn't react my mother said, "If I'd ever talked to you that way you'd have beat my ass!"

Granddaddy looked at me and said, "Maybe I ought to."

Then he told me to go lay on the bed. I had heard all the stories, and I was terrified he might really let me have it.

He came into the bedroom, and I was bent over on the bed holding my breath. I heard him pull the belt out of his pants and I squeezed my eyes closed bracing for the hit.

He leaned down and whispered, "You better scream, girl!" Then he walloped the bed! Whew!

From that moment forward our bond became even stronger.

I lived with my grandparents off and on during my early years, before David was born. After that, we would most likely end up at Ralph and Jean's house. Their son is only two months older than David, which made it more kid-friendly.

I loved Ralph and Jean and always felt safe with them. Having them as a safety net made all the difference for many years.

Over the summer between my junior and senior year in high school, when Les was finally out of our life, we moved into the house Ralph, and Jean had been renting in Toledo. They bought a house out near my grandparents in Holland, Ohio. Most of our belongings were in Ralph and Jean's house already since we had bounced back and forth before the time with Les was finally over.

Daddy duJour

Les' son went back to his mother in Georgia and, sadly we never saw him again. He was almost a teenager at the time, and I'm pretty sure his mother couldn't have him put in a home. Many years later I heard he had become a policeman. I could see that happening, and I'm sure he's a good one.

The duplex we had taken over from Ralph and Jean was just a few blocks from a very rough neighborhood. Over the summer of 1967, there were race riots that had moved down from Detroit and into other areas in Northwestern Ohio.

You could smell the smoke from the firebombs, especially at night. We didn't have air conditioning but, you didn't want to open the windows for many reasons. When we traveled in and out of the area, we had to drive around the perimeter of the riot zone to avoid trouble. You didn't dare walk alone. At least it wasn't during the school year. The worst of it was over within a few weeks, but nothing had been resolved.

It makes me sad and angry when I look back over the years and realize how many times I've witnessed or been near civil disruptions over race or other types of discrimination. Little did I know in 1967 how long it would go on or how bad it could get.

It seems it's been one step forward and two or three backward for a very long time.

It wasn't long before mom was talking about another guy. I kept hearing how wonderful 'Scotty' was. It was almost impossible to tune it out when she was around. Scotty was definitely on the hook.

I remember when I first met him face to face. I had spent the weekend with my friend, Nadine. The kids were with Ralph and Jean, and it was great to spend time just being a teenager. Nadine was driving me home, and I asked her to stop at the bar so I could get some money from mom, in case I needed to get groceries.

We walked into the bar, and Scotty happened to be there. He was not what I expected at all. He was short and a bit overweight and very jovial. He had bright blue eyes that seemed kind, unlike Les' ice blue ones.

He greeted Nadine and I with a hug after mom introduced us. It might have been a bit forward but, from that moment it felt like he had always been part of my life. At the very least it was, "Where have you been all my life?"

The second question was, "What do you see in my mother?"

He seemed so much better than that. But, I was and will always be grateful he came into our lives. He was there when I needed him most.

Chapter XIV
Scotty

Burns Woodward Scott married a woman whose father owned a funeral home. He then went to school to become a mortician, and after graduating, he went to work in the family business. They had two sons in a dysfunctional marriage. His wife had mental and emotional issues that became worse over time.

Scotty had moved into the apartment behind the funeral home across the street from the main house. His wife's psychological issues worsened, and she committed suicide. But, that was a few years after their divorce and before he met my mother.

Dead people scare me. I remember, while we were living with Marvin and Lorna, her aunt passed away. We all went to the funeral home, and I refused to go inside. Al was there, of course, it was his aunt, too. He tried to talk me into going in but, I planted myself firmly at the corner of the front porch of the funeral home.

After a while, Nancy, Al's other sister, came out and grabbed me by the hand and dragged me into the parlor with the open casket at the other end. I'm sure I was screaming, but it didn't stop her. She kept telling me to stop being a baby and promised me if I touched a dead person I would never be afraid again. It was a lie. I fainted.

So, having someone in my life, who worked with dead people regularly, was a conundrum. But, nothing about Scotty seemed funereal. He was always upbeat and singing, or whistling, a happy tune.

Having Scotty around made it easier for me to finish school without having to change districts again. He would come down to Toledo and pick me up every morning and drive me to school in Temperance, Michigan. I was so grateful for his generosity.

I took driver's ed during my junior year when we were still living with Les. Once we left Les, the only car we had was mom's beat up old '55 Chevy with Fred Flintstone floorboards. There was no way I could take the driver's test to get my license in that rust heap.

Scotty generously offered to let me take the test in his new Pontiac. It was more than generous of him and turned out to be one of many of his cars I banged up. We'll get to that in a moment.

I had been feeling very tired and weak for a while. We didn't have the healthiest of diets, but there was more to it than that. Our upstairs neighbor, Kim, told me her doctor had given her pills to keep her energy up and offered to give me one. She was pregnant, so I figured it must be safe, why not give it a try?

She brought me the pill around dinner time, and I took it right away. In a fairly short time, I was wired for sound!

Daddy duJour

I started scrubbing the entire house. Washing down walls and scrubbing the floors while singing at the top of my lungs to the radio.

I gave the kids a bath and tucked them into bed. Then I continued cleaning, while dancing, and singing. I'd never been so energized! I completely lost track of time and was surprised when mom came home from work. It was 2:00 am.

"What the hell got into you?" she asked.

"Kim gave me one of her pills for energy!" I said. "They really work!"

"I can see that," she said.

She poured herself a drink and checked out my work. It was spotless!

"We need to get to bed because you have to take your driving test tomorrow, remember?" she asked.

I had forgotten but, I wasn't the least bit tired and told her I'd be fine. She went off to bed, and I continued rearranging furniture and singing along with the radio.

Around 5am that all changed. I had to sit down. My head was spinning.

I passed out.

"Barb!" someone yelled, and I jumped. It was Scotty and mom was standing behind him looking at me shaking her head.

"What's wrong?" I asked.

"I told you we have to get you to your driving test, didn't I?" mom asked. "You should've come to bed."

"I couldn't sleep," I said.

"Do you feel up to going or do you want to reschedule?" Scotty asked.

I definitely didn't want to reschedule. I'd waited so long to get my license and losing a little sleep wasn't going to stop me. I jumped in the shower and tried to shake off the cloud over my head.

I got in the back seat of the car, and as we started up the street, I couldn't breathe.

"Can you put the windows down?" I asked.

"Are you ok?" Scotty asked.

"I really need some air," I said.

He put the windows down and then I couldn't catch my breath at all. We made a side trip to the E.R.

It turns out, in 1967, a pregnant woman could be given amphetamines. That's what was giving Kim all her energy and what knocked me out.

They discovered I was anemic and prescribed a series of shots and iron pills and told me never to take anyone else's medication again. It took a while for my system to get back in balance, and during that time there were some fainting spells.

After a doctors' visit for my last shot, I was feeling much better and stronger. Still had to take the iron pills daily but, I had more energy than I'd had in a long time. I asked mom if I could drive us home. I hadn't had much practice behind the wheel and needed some. She reluctantly said, "Yes," and handed me the keys. I still hadn't gotten my license, only a learners' permit.

The last time I had driven was in Scotty's Plymouth, not in the Fred Flintstone Chevy, so I'd forgotten how heavy and hard it was to steer. I was still weak, and I almost sideswiped a car. Mom made me stop. I didn't argue because I was afraid I might faint at any second. I kept the window down to get fresh air, which helped a little.

We stopped at the grocery store before going home, and I put the kids in the cart and started walking. Next thing I knew I was sitting on top of a stack of crates in the produce department with my head between my knees and a nice man was handing me a cold compress. Mom was yelling at me about how I could have killed us all if she hadn't made me stop driving. Her empathy was overwhelming.

I met Scotty's son, John, on my first day of school in Michigan while we were living with Les. John was a large, jovial guy who was in every school play, choir, glee club, everything all the time. He was Mr. Popularity!

As I was walking out of the principal's office with all my books, he came barreling around the corner, and we collided.

My books and papers went flying all over the hall. I wasn't hurt, only stunned. John immediately apologized and helped me up. We began picking everything up together. We got to know each other a bit after that, but we didn't run in the same circles. He was entrenched in music and theater at school and very popular. I was taking every art class available and had very few friends because babysitting kept me from after-school activities. But John was always friendly toward me. I hadn't met Scotty at that point, and even after I did, it took me a while to make the connection.

Eventually, I did get my driver's license and every morning Scotty would come to pick me up for school. It was about a forty-minute drive, and he always let me do the driving while he napped. In the funeral business, there is no nine to five, so he was happy to nap. It was fun for me, and I needed a lot of practice.

One morning we were running late, and when we reached the intersection at school, I took the corner a little too fast and the car skid in the gravel, slamming into some poor woman's car door. Scotty immediately woke up and assessed the situation, while the woman I hit was wanting to kill me, I was sure. He got out and introduced himself to the woman, and with a smile on his face said to me, "You run along, you don't want to be late, I'll take care of this."

That was his demeanor all the time. Positive, and rarely flustered by anything. It was a personality type I was not used to but grew to love and admire more than I can say.

He did, in fact, take care of everything and we never spoke of it again. And, we didn't tell my mother.

Daddy duJour

There were a couple of other incidents, (accidents), with his cars, too.

One time I got sick at school and began vomiting. The nurse told me to call a parent to pick me up because I couldn't go back to class. So, I called Scotty. He was close-by, and I knew he would be there for me.

This time he came in his vintage 1955 Cadillac, which technically belonged to the funeral home. He came to the nurse's office, and we went straight out the front door to the car. As soon as we started to move I knew I was going to throw-up but, I couldn't get the words out before the vomit.

They were never able to get the smell out of the car. I've always felt horrible about that. It was worth a lot of money before that day. I can only imagine what it might be worth now if I hadn't ruined it.

Then there was the time I went to pick-up my altered prom dress in Scotty's new Pontiac.

Yes, I did get to go to the junior prom while we were still with Les. I didn't have many friends at school, so I wasn't surprised at not being asked. One of my friends was a guy named Gary who sat behind me in History class. He was on the football team, which I had no interest in, and had been dating the same girl for a couple of years so, obviously, he had a date.

Gary was surprised to hear I hadn't been asked. I told him it was no big deal, really. Although I had done a large portion of the décor for the prom, along with other art students, I didn't really care if I went or not.

But, Gary thought this was all wrong, and I should go to the prom, so he put a sign in the boy's locker room:

Attention! Twig has no date for the prom! Who's going to fix that?

Yes, that was my nickname in that high school, Twig. I was about the same size as the model, Twiggy, and that's where it came from.

So, a few days before the prom a guy in my English class slipped me a note and asked if I would go to the prom with him. He was kind of nerdy and shy, but nice. I thought, why not!

Mom took me shopping for a dress the next day. We found a soft pink chiffon number with cutaway shoulders and a high neck. When you're called Twig, it's pretty obvious you have no cleavage.

I was really looking forward to the big night. I'd never attended a school dance in my seventeen years. Aside from the few kids, I knew from art class that were going, and Gary and his girlfriend, I really knew no one.

Two days before the prom my date broke his foot! He came to school with a cast halfway up his leg. I couldn't believe it. But, he insisted the date was still on. He was brave.

Obviously, there was no dancing for us, but it was nice to see the fruits of my labors in the gym and to appreciate what a gentleman I came with. Sad to say, I can't even remember his name!

Daddy duJour

Back at the scene of the crime.

I was driving Scotty's new Pontiac and had my brothers in the back seat. They were five and nine years old.

The woman who did the prom dress alterations lived on a busy street, and she told me, over the phone, to come around back through the alley, and she would bring the dress out to me. I managed to get the car up the alley but, it was a tight fit. The '67 Pontiac was a large car.

I picked up the dress, and drove out the other end of the alley and turned to head back to the busy street. As I waited to pull out at the corner of the busy street a pick-up truck was trying to turn into the side street but, I was out too far. So, I put it in reverse and let my foot off the brake popping backward into another car's grill. I hadn't even touched the gas.

I got out to check the damage and the driver of the Ford Fairlane I had just crushed the grill of was not a happy guy. There was no damage to Scotty's car at all. I tried to explain to the man what happened, it was clearly my fault for not looking in the rear view mirror but, I only took my foot off the brake. He did not care. He wanted the owner's info, which I went and got out of the glove compartment.

I got back in the car, shaking like a leaf. It didn't help that the boys were yelling, "Mom's gonna kill you!" like a chant.

I drove straight to the funeral home to report to Scotty. By the time I got there he had already spoken to the guy I had hit. No time was wasted for that news flash! This was long before cell phones, too. But, Scotty came out humming a tune, something he regularly did while filling his pipe.

"So, I hear you had a little accident," he said.

Lord, when I think about my history with his cars and how cool, calm and collected he was, it amazes me to this day. He took care of everything and told the boys never to speak of it to mom. Amazingly they obeyed. He may have bribed them, which wouldn't surprise me.

Scotty always knew how to defuse the tension between my mother and me. Aside from my grandparents and my uncle Ralph and his wife, Jean, Scotty was my greatest and dearest advocate and ally.

In addition to the kindness and fun Scotty brought to my life, he introduced me to reading for pleasure. I had always enjoyed the required reading for school but, aside from the trashy novels Al used to keep around, we didn't have books in our house.

The first book Scotty ever gave me was Rosemary's Baby. I was home alone with the boys one night and started reading it as soon as I put them to bed. I couldn't put it down. Just about the time I reached the startling climax of the story I heard, "Boo!"

I'm pretty sure I levitated off the chair. It was Scotty, who I hadn't even heard come in. At that moment I wanted to throw the book at him, but we both ended up laughing.

Chapter XV
Moving On

My mother was still working at the truck stop bar when her divorce was final from Les. The house in Michigan was sold, and she wasn't on the deed, so in keeping true to form, Les gave her nothing from the sale. We hadn't lived there for quite a while, and her commute to work from my uncle's old duplex was quite a distance.

Scotty helped mom find a three-bedroom house closer to work and big enough for everyone. He even had his own room. I knew they had intimate relations but, never when I was around.

The boys had their own room, and I shared the master bedroom with mom. It sounds more awkward than it really was. Being on call for the funeral home, Scotty would be in and out of the house at all hours of the day and night, so he needed his own room.

Having Scotty around was a blessing for me. He was great with the boys and would take them to the movies or just spend time with them and relieve me of babysitting.

He took me to my first off-Broadway play, 'Hello Dolly' starring Dorothy Lamour! I'd seen school productions but never a Broadway road show. Scotty loved music and theater. He brought culture into my life. I am forever grateful.

Once in a while, I would go to the Toledo Museum of Art by myself. It often seemed I never had any time alone and there was something very spiritual about being in the Cloister Gallery at the museum. It reminded me of Romeo and Juliet, which had been required reading at one of the schools I attended. Sitting alone there stirred my soul and encouraged my art.

Before we moved into the new place, Scotty introduced me to one of the guys who worked weekends at the funeral home driving the ambulance/hearse. His name was Chris. He was from Toronto and going to Toledo University.

Chris and his roommate, Dave, would go to hospitals or morgues and pick up the bodies. Then deliver them to the funeral home. Sometimes they would help Scotty with whatever needed to be done at the funeral home.

Chris had asked me out a couple of times but, I declined. He didn't appeal to me at all. Then one day he came by with his roommate, Dave. I thought Dave was very cute.

I had cookies in the oven, and they followed me to the kitchen. When I took the cookies out Dave said, "They're not done." I believe I said, "Thank you, Betty Crocker." And so, it began. Sarcasm was something we had in common.

Dave's brother-in-law had just been killed in Viet Nam, and he was heading home to Massachusetts for the funeral in a couple of days. It was December, and I

Daddy duJour

thought how awful that would be for the family. A Christmas you could never forget.

When Dave came back to Toledo, we had moved to the larger house, and he came out with Chris. We were still getting settled, there were unpacked boxes everywhere, and the stove wasn't working. Dave took a look and figured out it was the gas connection. It was probably a quick fix, but he managed to stretch it out a week or so which meant coming out to the house each night. Without fail, Chris would be five minutes behind him.

We would play card games, or Parcheesi and listen to the stereo. It was fun and relaxing, and often Scotty would be there with us. It was January 1968, and there was so much to talk about. Chris, being Canadian, wasn't all that involved in our politics but, Scotty and Dave and I were.

We discussed where we were and what we felt when JFK was shot. I can't imagine anyone could forget where they were and how they felt that day. I was in 8th grade English class when the announcement came over the PA system. It was a large junior high school, and I swear you could hear a pin drop throughout the building.

Dave, of course, had the raw emotions of his brother-in-law being killed in Viet Nam. He was not a Nixon fan in any way; even though, his parents were Republicans.

Those discussions would lead to talk of LBJ and the Republican and Democratic conventions. No one was pro-Nixon in these discussions, that's for sure. We all know how that turned out, don't we?

Barbara Hammond

At the end of the evening, I'd be waiting for Chris to leave so I could have some time alone with Dave. I finally had to tell Chris outright I had no interest in dating him.

After Chris got the message, he stopped coming every time but would show up occasionally. Dave seemed shy, at first, and I began to think he really wasn't interested in me.

Then, finally, one night as I walked him to the door he stopped and kissed me. That was it. I'd never felt that way before. If he hadn't been holding me tight, my knees would have buckled, and I would have fallen to the floor.

Mom would never let me go to a drive-in on a date before Dave. After all the things I had been exposed to by her behavior with men, it was the ultimate irony that she was concerned about my virginity. Dave had a little sports car, a Triumph Spitfire, so she saw no problem with that. She would have been very surprised.

Chapter XVI

Mark and Nadine

During the Les years, I met a guy who lived around the corner from us before we moved to Michigan. He was a senior, and I was a sophomore. He sent his younger sister out to ask my name as I walked by their house one day.

I was taken aback and asked who her brother was. She said his name was Mark. I told her if he wanted to know my name he could ask me himself. I kept walking.

The next day, as I walked by their house, he pulled out of the driveway in an old beat up car. I'm pretty sure he had been sitting there, with the car idling, waiting for me to come down the street. He rolled the window down and said, "Hi there!"

I said hello and kept walking. He followed alongside me and asked my name.

"Oh, you're the guy who sent your kid sister out to ask me that yesterday?"

"Yeah, that's right," he said.

"My name's Barbara, what's yours?"

"Mark," he said.

I kept walking, and he crawled along next to me in his car. When I got to my house, I headed for the door and waved goodbye to Mark.

"Hey! Wait a minute," he said, "Don't you want to go for a ride or something?"

I looked at him shaking my head and said, "ah, NO."

"Oh, you're one of those kinda girls," he said.

I walked into the house.

He was kind of cute but had way too much attitude. Cockiness isn't a trait I admire. Sending your little sis out to do your bidding? I thought he was a loser.

He was, however, very persistent.

This would be a good time to tell you more about my closest friend, Nadine.

When my uncle Ralph met Jean, she was divorced. And, even though she left her husband, she didn't leave the relationships she had with his family. Her mother-in-law, Denna, knew it was her son's fault the marriage failed and kept a very close relationship with Jean. So did Denna's sisters, Delsey, Delma and Darcy. Weird. I know.

There was a very tight bond between the sisters and Jean. They welcomed Ralph into the fold and ostracized their own, who moved to West Virginia and wasn't heard from again.

After Jean married my uncle, we all became friends with her former in-laws. She introduced me to Delma's

Daddy duJour

daughter, Nadine, when I was about seven years old, and Nadine was eight. We became fast friends despite living in completely different parts of town. With all the schools I attended, (fourteen in twelve years), Nadine's was in a district I never lived in.

At the time we met, my mother was married to Al and David hadn't been born yet. Ralph and Jean would take me across town for overnight visits with Nadine. I always looked forward to it.

They lived in a small Tudor-style house that had a finished basement. There was even a small kitchenette in the basement which made it perfect for pretending we had our own apartments.

We never played house, in the traditional way. We pretended we were single women with our own apartments and careers. She was 'Elliott,' a doctor in charge of the local hospital, and I was 'Ellen,' a reporter for the local paper. Funny how those make-believe roles ended up being close to true.

Oh, the scenarios we played out! So much imagination went into our play dates. We had 'dates' with guys, of course, but, no intention of giving up our careers for marriage. So ahead of our time! We're talking late 50's, into early '60's.

(It's interesting that she ended up the head nurse in an AIDS ward, and I write. Never underestimate a child's imagination or intention.)

We didn't see each other much during the trailer park times but, after mom and Al got back together before

Tim was born, we started getting together again. We were both in our teens then, and things had changed for both of us.

Her folks had divorced, and we didn't have our 'apartments' to play in anymore. But, whenever possible we would catch up at Ralph and Jean's house.

Nadine never liked Mark, the guy who sent his sister out to get my name. She saw right through him. He wasn't a big fan of hers either. Mark was short, about 5'5", Nadine was 5'9" and never let him forget it. She never missed an opportunity to throw a short joke his way.

In hindsight, Mark was a dick. He deserved it.

One night, when Nadine was staying overnight at my house, Mark came over. We had been seeing each other but not really dating, so he would just come and hang out at our house almost every night. He lived right around the corner.

Nadine and I were baking a cake and listening to music out in the kitchen. I needed a plate that was on the top shelf in the cabinet and pulled a kitchen chair over to get up to reach it.

Mark said, "You're no taller than my little brother, and you're built like him, too."

That's all it took for Nadine to tower over him, as he sat in the chair, and eviscerate him. I don't recall her exact words, but 'little dick' was in there somewhere.

He got up and left.

Daddy duJour

That night she said, "What the hell do you see in him?"

I didn't have an answer. We never really went on a date. I guess he was a distraction from the crazy world of Les, and the fact that Les didn't like him was a bonus.

Shortly after Les surprised us all with news of a house in Michigan that we would 'all be happy in,' things got more serious with Mark.

The way to get your kids to do the exact opposite of what you want them to do is to make it forbidden fruit. Once we were settled in the new house and I was into my junior year in the new high school, Les decided I was never to see Mark again. Mom was on board with this, as well. She didn't like Mark but, more importantly, she wanted to stay on Les' good side

As much as Nadine hated Mark, she became our social secretary. All of our meetings were arranged through her, except the times Mark would wait for Les to leave and then show up at the back door.

One of those nights I heard the tapping at our sliding glass door shortly after the kids went to bed and there was Mark. There were no cell phones then and I didn't expect to see him that night.

"What are you doing here?" I asked.

"I'm thinking about joining the Army," he said.

"What??"

This was at the height of the Viet Nam War. He felt sure he would be drafted and thought if he joined it might be easier. It wasn't uncommon at that time.

As soon as I let him in, I heard Les' car in the garage. Mark ran out the back, and I plopped myself in front of the TV.

"Where is he?!" Les demanded.

"Where's who?" I asked.

"You know damn well who I'm talking about," he said.

Well, I was in my flannel nightgown with brush rollers in my hair, so I figured that was pretty good defense on its own. But, he insisted on searching the house and waking the kids in the process. Then he got in his car, and I was hoping Mark would be out of the neighborhood before Les saw him.

A little while later Les came back home and went straight to bed. I decided it was best if I broke up with Mark. It was more of a spite relationship, really. I had no feelings for him; I simply wanted to defy Les and mom. Now it was all getting on my nerves, and he wasn't worth it.

Not long after that night came the beatings from Les that changed everything. We had moved to my uncle's house, and Mark was the last thing on my mind but, he began pleading with Nadine to 'talk sense to me.' He must have forgotten that she never liked him in the first place. But, somehow he convinced her he really loved me and wanted me back and asked for her help in arranging a New Year's Eve date.

Daddy duJour

"Come on, it's just one night," she said.

I knew she simply wanted this to be the end of Mark and figured if I went along with his plan I could convince him it was over. It wouldn't be the first time I had spent New Year's Eve with her so no one would question my staying with her for the night.

There was so much drama at home with the divorce and the kids, because we still had Les' son, and weren't sure how that would play out. I decided to go along and get away for a couple of days.

Mark picked me up at Nadine's house, and we drove an hour out to Whitehouse, Ohio, which is right next to Waterville where David and I had lived with Al's sister and husband.

The party was at a fire hall, so common in that area, and we were clearly the youngest people there. We met up with the couple Mark had been friends with so, at least we weren't completely alone in a sea of old folks.

About halfway to midnight, a man tapped me on the shoulder and when I turned around my mouth dropped to the floor. It was Marvin, Al's brother-in-law!

"What are you doing here?" He asked.

"My date brought me. What are you doing here?"

"Well it is the next town over, you know."

Actually, I didn't know. The area we were in didn't resemble Waterville, to me, so I hadn't made that connection. He led me over to say hello to Lora. It was a very chilly moment standing there with the guy who had tried to molest me, and the woman who tried to turn me over to my father so she could keep my little brother.

I said my hellos and walked back to Mark's table.

"Who are those people?" he asked.

"Old step-relatives."

"Can we go now?" I asked.

"It's not even midnight yet," he said.

"I really don't care. I'm not feeling well, and this was a mistake," I said.

I knew he was pissed but, I was having a fight or flight moment and didn't think I could have gotten a cab out in the hinterlands. He must have seen the determination on my face and began saying his goodbyes to his friends. I tried to be gracious about it, but deep down I knew I would never see anyone in the entire room again after that night. It was a long cold and quiet ride back to Nadine's house.

Chapter XIX
Dave

Often, on the weekends, if mom wasn't working the four of us, Mom, Scotty, Dave and I would hang out at the house and play cards. Scotty always made things more relaxed. It was just his way.

Scotty made life bearable in so many ways. The boys loved him, and he loved them like his own. His schedule was erratic but, if he was home in the evening when mom was working and Dave and I wanted to go out, it was no problem.

One night in March, or maybe it was April, Dave and I went to the movies, and when we got home, Scotty ran out to the car to warn me that mom was on the warpath. Somehow she had discovered who I was with on New Year's Eve.

It seems Marvin, who I'd had the pleasure of running into on New Year's Eve, had shown up at the bar where mom was working. He didn't know she would be there but, they had lots to talk about, especially since he had recently seen me.

Mom was taking a bath so, we got ourselves something to drink and sat down at the kitchen table waiting for the big show. It was really something. I can't remember it verbatim but, it went something like this...

"So, Dave, you probably don't know she's been cheating on you, do you?"

No time for a response as she ranted on.

"She lied to me, so I'm sure she's lied to you, too. She said she was staying with Nadine but, she spent New Year's Eve with her old boyfriend, Mark."

Dave said nothing. We all sat silently waiting for her to go on with the show.

I don't remember it all but, I know she went out of her way to portray me in her own likeness. A cheap whore.

Dave and I hardly knew each other until January and didn't go on an actual date for at least a month, maybe longer. He was kind of shy in the beginning but, we were definitely attracted to each other.

We spent most of our time listening to music and discussing world affairs. It was a very eventful year, 1968. Often Scotty would be hanging out with us, and that always made conversation even more interesting.

When mom was home we would most likely be playing cards, Hearts usually. She was never that interested in world affairs. After a while, Dave would bring an overnight bag on the weekends and crash in Scotty's room. It was an odd arrangement, for sure, but it was fine with me.

We let mom rant for a while longer and then told her Dave already knew how I spent New Year's Eve. It completely deflated her and deservedly so. I couldn't understand why she was so nasty and vindictive. She liked Dave, why would she want that relationship destroyed?

There's no explaining my mother. If anything, mom's rant brought Dave and me closer.

The following weekend Scotty asked Dave and me if we would mind driving up to Ann Arbor to pick up his son, John, at the University of Michigan. We didn't mind at all. I loved John and Dave was fine with getting away. Time away was always a plus. He handed Dave the keys, and we were on our way.

Dave was the first guy I truly enjoyed talking to. When I think about conversations with Mark, it makes me laugh. He was critical and, honestly, a chauvinist with a Napoleon complex.

Dave and I were both interested in politics and world affairs and never lacked for interesting things to discuss. Maybe we didn't always agree but, that's what made it more interesting.

On the way up to Ann Arbor, we made a pit stop for gas and to use the restrooms. When we got in the car to head back out Dave reached into his pocket and said, "Here, I got you something."

It was a huge fake diamond ring he'd gotten out of a vending machine! We had a good laugh over that, but it made me think of the possibilities. We were friends first, and that was something I was unfamiliar with, as far as men were concerned and mom's experiences.

Barbara Hammond

My mother never had conversations with any men I knew of that stretched from world affairs to art, from politics to baseball. With Dave I always looked forward to those discussions.

I once flew on a six-passenger Piper with my grandparents when I was twelve from Toledo, Ohio to Rome, GA. An old friend of my Uncle Chuck's from his Korean War days was a pilot. He loved my grandparents and offered them a free trip to visit family down south, and I got to go along. I played the Stewardess as I handed out the sandwiches my grandmother had packed for the trip.

It was fun. But, I'd never been on a commercial jet until I flew to Boston with Dave to meet his family over Easter break. I had traveled back and forth between Ohio and Georgia at least once a year for most of my life but, with the exception of the one small plane flight, it was all by car.

So, as we began the approach to Logan Airport, I had another first, seeing the Atlantic Ocean. I was seventeen and had grown up along Lake Erie but, I'd never seen an ocean. It was exhilarating! Unlike meeting the parents. That was kind of intimidating.

They were very nice, don't get me wrong, and their home reminded me of Minnie and Delmar's where I stayed when I was five. Spotlessly clean, warm and inviting. It felt like a home.

Daddy duJour

Dave's sister had been living back home since the death of her husband in Viet Nam in December. She was a bit stand-offish, but she was still mourning.

Dave and I went shopping at Jordan Marsh on Saturday. His mom gave him her credit card so he could get some things he needed for the spring semester. I had brought some of my own money, thanks to Scotty, and found a gorgeous wide brimmed hat that went perfectly with the dress I'd brought to wear on Easter Sunday. I had enough to pay for the hat and some leftover for souvenirs. Nevermind that the hat was unbelievably impractical! I think we had to check it in its own box on the way back home. But, it was the perfect Easter Bonnet.

Going to Dave's parent's Episcopal church that Easter was quite different than some of my childhood church memories. It was peaceful and calming, unlike what I'd been exposed to.

All in all, it was a lovely visit, and I felt comfortable with Dave's family. I think they approved of me, as well. I worried a bit about how they would feel when they met my mother. I always worried about what others would think when they met her.

Back in Toledo mom was having some health issues, and her doctor scheduled her for a hysterectomy. She'd had four children by cesarean section, and it had taken a toll. Today her procedure would have been an overnight hospital stay but, in May of 1968, it was a five-day event. Mom made it eventful.

Barbara Hammond

I was staying home from school to take care of the boys. My senior year was primarily art classes, with English and Government on the side. Plus, I was working on my first oil painting to be presented in the class art show so, the time at home was helpful.

Still, taking care of young boys is always challenging and often messy. I was cleaning the house, in my pajamas, the day before mom was due home when Dave stopped by. I was a mess. Literally.

"What brings you by in the middle of the day?" I asked.

He reached into his pocket and pulled out a ring. It wasn't in a box. It was between his thumb and forefinger. I thought it was another joke.

"What cracker jack box did you get that one out of?" I asked.

He looked crushed! I took the ring from his hand and realized it was real. Talk about a romantic moment?! Not so much. I felt like a fool and apologized. He pulled me into his arms, and we held each other tight.

It felt like we had been together forever. I had never been that comfortable with any other man in my life. Kismet, I suppose you could say.

I was excited to go see mom at the hospital and tell her the good news. She was not impressed. Suddenly Dave was the enemy, and all she saw was her built-in childcare drifting away. Scotty, on the other hand, was thrilled for us.

Daddy duJour

The Art Show at school was the week before graduation. I had worked so hard on this painting and had such mixed emotions about it. I took the image from a TIME magazine cover photo of an infant in all white lace lying on a white lace pillow. I don't remember what the photo was about. I just felt compelled to paint it. White on white is not easy to paint. But, I was feeling fairly confident about the finished painting.

My art teacher raved about it, which made me happy but, I was doubtful it would sell. Who would buy a painting of a baby they didn't know? The mother of one of my classmates, that's who. I don't remember how much it sold for. It didn't matter to me. I just wanted it back. I offered to buy it back, and she wouldn't do it. I have no photo of it, either. I knew I would never paint anything that good again.

Fortunately, I have continued to paint over the years. I've sold my work, too, and still, I wish I'd kept that one.

The evening of my high school graduation mom wasn't feeling well enough to attend. So she said. She'd been home from the hospital for a few weeks and seemed fine, but going to the graduation of her daughter, who would be the first one in her entire family to graduate from high school wasn't important to her. It hurt.

But, I had the love and support of my favorite people, Dave, Nadine and her mom, Delma, and Scotty.

When we returned home, mom was sitting at the kitchen table playing cards with one of her girlfriends, smokin', jokin', and drinking. I've never forgiven her for that slight. There's a long list of things I've not been able to forgive her for.

Once school was out, I began looking for a job. The big problem was, it had to align with mom's schedule, and that made it next to impossible. She wanted me home to watch the kids when she went to work at the bar at 4 pm.

I wanted to work for an advertising agency. My art background, feeble as it was, would be helpful and I had a connection with a friend who suggested I take an internship at an agency in town. Without a college degree, it would have been a long ladder to climb but, I was ready willing and able. Mom wouldn't hear of it. It didn't fit her schedule.

A friend from high school was working at a Big Boy's restaurant, and they needed someone to take her shift when she went to college in September. But, I wouldn't get home in time to watch the kids, so mom killed that idea.

However, she did come home with a great idea for me that would work for her.

Sunoco was running an ad campaign on TV with young girls pumping gas in hot pants. Mom talked to the guy at our local Sunoco station about hiring me to pump gas in hot pants, just like on TV! He was all in.

Dave happened to be at the house when she came home with this great news. She went on and on about how perfect it was, and most importantly it wouldn't disrupt her schedule for me, her babysitter.

Daddy duJour

I wanted to choke her. She thought I was an ungrateful bitch. Dave said, "What kind of mother would rather have her daughter pumping gas in hot pants than working at a respectable ad agency or waiting tables in a family restaurant?"

"See, you're not even married to the son of a bitch yet, and he's trying to run your life!" she said.

"Whose life is it anyway?" I shrieked.

Chapter XVII

Moving On

As my future seemed stuck in Toledo, Dave's dad, who was a store manager for the S.S.Kresge Co., was transferred to the Pittsburgh, PA area to manage a new Kmart store. We drove out to visit and to tell them we were engaged.

Dave had decided to leave college and join the S.S.Kresge Co. like his dad. The company had been good to his dad and was expanding widely with Kmart stores opening all over, so we had that news to share, as well.

Since I'd met them at Easter and stayed in their home, I wasn't nervous about this trip but, still not sure how they would take two big news items during one dinner.

This was 1968 and wearing white gloves was not unusual for going to church or a special event but, having dinner in the dining room of a Holiday Inn was not quite the same. None the less I kept my white gloves on until it seemed the right time to expose the ring. Dave's mom was not fooled one bit!

As it turned out, they were fine with the engagement but, not as much about Dave leaving college. I know they wanted both of their children to have a college education. Most parents want their children to have a better life than they had. My mother, on the other hand,

Daddy duJour

wouldn't have cared one way or the other if I had quit high school. Education was not a priority in my family.

We were feeling pretty positive about things as we made our way back to Toledo. It would take Dave some time to wrap up his classes and prepare to move. He was able to start his management training close to his parent's house in Butler, PA. Close enough to commute, anyway.

As we drove back after dinner, we felt things had gone better than expected. Now we had to push the waitressing job on my mother and hope Scotty could back me up.

He tried as best he could to make her understand it was time for me to go and live my life but, she didn't care. She blamed Dave for tearing me away and was furious with Scotty for taking my side.

After Dave's folks settled into their new home in Butler, they asked if they could come out to meet my mother and Scotty. I couldn't say no but, I really wanted to. Dave's mother was the polar opposite of mine. I was dreading the meeting.

We made arrangements to go out to dinner, the six of us, and before we left, I made the mistake of asking, no, pleading with mom to go easy with the swearing and not embarrass me. Dumb move on my part.

My mother cussed like a sailor. Dave's mom would spell Hell, H E double hockey sticks!. You could not find two women more opposite of each other. It was a difficult night for me but, Dave's parents seemed to be understanding and that was a relief.

Dave's parents, Gordon and Sally, each had very difficult childhoods. They were both given up by their mothers' to relatives at an early age. In Gordon's situation, he became a hired hand at a farm in the Catskills. I use hired in a loose sense because he wasn't paid. It was very much like enslavement.

Sally was given to an aunt in Pelham, NY, when she was quite young. She became the primary caregiver to that aunt, over time. Even caring for her long distance after she'd married and had children of her own.

They understood my parental relationship better than anyone. It helped us bond and, I was grateful.

When I couldn't make my mother understand I was not her slave and had to live my own life, Dave and I decided I should move to Butler, and until I could find a job and get my own apartment, I could stay at his parent's home. They were gracious enough to agree.

Dave had been living with them since he started the management training program in July. He was putting a lot of miles on his Triumph Spitfire, crossing the PA and Ohio turnpikes at least once a week.

Scotty was my rock. He assured me the kids would be taken care of and I need not worry about them. As badly as I wanted my freedom, I felt like I was abandoning my own children. Stressful doesn't begin to describe those few days before I left.

I made arrangements with Nadine to move some of my things to her house that I couldn't take, in one trip, especially in Dave's little car. She was happy to help. In all our years as friends, she knew better than anyone what this would be like.

When we came back from Nadine's and began loading the rest of my things in Dave's car Scotty threw me a curve.

"You can't leave before your mother gets home," he said.

"What are you talking about? I do not want to deal with that showdown," I said.

"If you're going out on your own and leaving your family you have to tell her to her face," he said.

I couldn't argue, although I wanted to in the worst way. This was not going to be easy. Plus it wasn't even dark yet, and she wouldn't be home until at least eleven o'clock.

The kids had seen us packing Dave's car and knew I was leaving. They just didn't know where I was going or when I'd be back. Scotty was there to assure them everything would be ok and he would take care of them. He wanted them to be happy for me. But, there was no happy in that house that night.

"So, I hear you're taking a little trip," she said.

I don't remember my response. I'm not sure she even gave me time to respond. She went directly onto the tirade I had anticipated.

She was screaming and cursing, and I tuned out. All I wanted was to get out of there and as far away from her as I could. Then she said, "You walk out that door, and you are dead to me. You will never see your brothers again! Do you understand me?"

I looked at Scotty, and he was shaking his head, as if to say, "Don't worry about that, I'll take care of things."

I knew he would but, I was worried about what she would tell the boys. They were four and eight years old and had been through so much already in their short lives. Her first instinct would be to turn them against me. It was all black and white in her demented mind. But, I also knew I had to make the break.

The kids had gone to bed long before she came home and I told them I was going away for a while. I made them promise to behave and listen to Scotty. They were wary of what was going on. Kids are very instinctual. But, I had to trust that everything would be all right once the dust settled.

I had been their primary caregiver for most of their lives. If not for Scotty I honestly don't know if I could have left them. But we hugged and kissed and hugged some more. Then I tucked them in for the night.

Chapter XVIII

Starting a New Life

After mom's threat to keep me away from my brothers and Scotty's nod for us to go, Dave and I drove away and headed to Butler, PA. I don't remember much conversation during that trip. We were both exhausted physically and emotionally.

Dave's parents were sound asleep when we slipped in. What was intended to be his sister's room was all prepared with crisp linens and a warm comforter.

Claudia had left for a European trip with some of her sorority sisters. She was still trying to figure out what came next after losing her husband in the Viet Nam war. I doubted she would be living in Butler for long, once she returned.

I was grateful for a warm bed and immediately fell asleep.

The next morning I smelled coffee brewing and was surprised when I looked at the clock on the nightstand. It was after 10am, and I knew Dave had left for work by then, so it would just be Sally and me for breakfast.

Sally was such a sweet soul. She reminded me of Minnie, the lovely woman who took care of me when I was five.

Their homes were designed and run the same. Very much like what you would see on a 1950's TV show.

Mamaw was a great cook but, she wasn't the best housekeeper. Sally was the wife I aspired to be. However, our personalities were quite different, and Dave was not like his dad at all.

Over coffee, in the morning, Sally and I would talk about our childhoods. Hers was not like a storybook either. Ironically, she and Gordon had very similar childhoods with absentee parents, both of them were raised by other relatives. I'm certain that's what created our instant bond. They understood my life, to a point, and were there to help.

While I was still searching for a job and my own apartment, Sally and I enjoyed sharing stories in the morning when the guys left for work. Her upbringing was quite different from mine. She and Gordon were only children. They had no siblings but, a few cousins.

The reason her home reminded me of Minnie's was that she was raised that way by her aunt. Very prim and proper. I wondered what my childhood would have been like if I'd continued living with Minnie and Delmar. I'll never know.

In the vein of 'prim and proper,' I remember one night Dave came home late and his parents had gone to bed. I was in my nightgown, and we were lying on the living room floor listening to the stereo.

Daddy duJour

No clothes were removed, just listening to music and planning our life together. We fell asleep in each other's arms.

We woke when we heard Gordon get up. I waited for him to go into the bathroom before I ducked into the bedroom.

Before Dave left for work, Sally had a talk with him. She believed him that we were not doing anything wrong, and knew we would never do that in her living room, but, "What if the mailman had come to the door and seen you like that?"

We still laugh when we think about it.

In a short time, I found a job at the Howard Johnson's in downtown Butler, working at the counter. It was a busy place but didn't provide enough income to afford an apartment.

Dave chipped in for an efficiency apartment a block away from the restaurant. It was small but fit my needs. He was still sleeping at his parent's house, but that's about all the time he spent there.

We agreed that we should go back to Toledo to get the rest of my things from Nadine's on Dave's next day off. There wasn't a lot to get, and it was mostly clothes. But, I also wanted my easel and art supplies.

When we got into Toledo, I immediately called Scotty to see how the boys were doing and hoping I might be able to see them. He threw me a curve.

"Why don't you come to the house and see them," he said.

Well, it was mom's day off, and I didn't want another showdown. But, when I told him that he said, "You'll be surprised."

"Will you be there?" I asked. He assured me he would.

We drove to the house full of trepidation and a bit of hope. So many things were going through my mind as I prepared for a confrontation. But, Dave kept reassuring me we would turn around and leave if that happened again.

The boys came running out to meet us, with Scotty following behind them. I hugged them all, and we went inside.

Mom was in the living room in the same chair as the last time we spoke. She got up and came over to give me a hug. I stiffened a bit, never knowing what might come next. She gave Dave a hug and asked about his new job and how we liked Pennsylvania. It was as if nothing out of the ordinary had ever happened in that very living room a few short weeks before.

It hadn't taken all that long for her to find a babysitter, after all. I'm sure Scotty vetted this person, so it wasn't like Mary, Darryl, and Darryl, several years before. Somehow they were able to survive without a free built-in housekeeper and nanny. No surprise to me.

We didn't stay all that long but, it was so nice to see the boys were doing well and Scotty had kept his promise.

Not that I ever doubted him but, when you're dealing with a bipolar personality, like mom, you can never be certain things won't fall apart suddenly and unexpectedly.

Of course, I didn't know what bipolar was back then but, I knew she was unstable. She was also an alcoholic. Not a fun combination to live with. God bless Burns W. Scott for being in my life when I needed an ally. Not to mention, he introduced me to Dave, and my life was becoming my own.

As Dave and I drove back to PA, we were much more relaxed. It was time to put our energies into our life together.

Chapter XIX

A Surprise Wedding

We got back to Butler rather late after stopping on the turnpike to grab a bite to eat. Both of us were exhausted but, feeling more at peace. After the car was unloaded, Dave went straight to his parents home. He had to go to work early in the morning.

Dave was in his third month of management training, and it seemed to be going smoothly. He came to the apartment after work one evening and told me they were transferring him to Uniontown, PA as an assistant manager. It was quite a coup to get a promotion that soon in his training.

It would be just under two hours each way but, he was willing to get a room there and commute back to Butler the night before his day off and Saturday nights because the stores weren't open on Sundays back then.

The company was growing by leaps and bounds in 1968, and those in management who were good at their job were being moved up the corporate ladder rather quickly. We figured his time in Uniontown would be short.

The week after the sudden transfer news I heard Dave at the door around 11pm. He came in and said, "We're going to be married before the week is over."

I just stared at him in disbelief. I'm sure my mouth was open, but no words were coming out. He said, "They rescinded my transfer to Uniontown, and they're sending me to Scarsdale, NY!"

I couldn't speak. My head was spinning. I had to sit down.

"I'm not going alone!" he said.

Well, I certainly didn't want him leaving me in Butler, PA alone but, it was such an overwhelming moment I couldn't think straight.

Dave and I had tried eloping once, shortly after I got my apartment in Butler. I honestly can't remember why we were rushing it but, it became a moot point.

Someone told us you could get married at 18 years of age in West Virginia without a parent's consent, so we decided to try it. It was not far, and we could do it on a Saturday that Dave got out of work early. Seemed like a simple plan but, when we got there, we discovered that was not true.

We were told the closest state that didn't require a parent's signature for someone under 21 was Indiana. Clearly, we couldn't get back on the road and head further west, so we gave up and went back to my apartment to figure out plan B.

With the transfer coming up within a couple of weeks, we didn't have a lot of time to plan. Dave went home and told his folks what was happening. They took it well.

I know his dad was proud that they were moving Dave along so quickly.

Since the plan was to go to Indiana for the wedding, I decided to call my mother and ask her if she and Scotty would like to come with us. We had to go through Ohio to get to Indiana. It made sense, but, she said, "Why not get married here in Toledo?" When I explained, she said, "If I sign for you, you can get married here!"

I hadn't given that any thought but, it would be much simpler and faster. This wedding was 'on the fly'!

The next morning we hit the road for Toledo. I packed a couple of dress choices and a few accessories but, none of those things were what I would have chosen had there been time to shop.

As soon as we arrived, mom told us we had to go to the courthouse and get the paperwork filled out. There was one big glitch when we got there. She didn't know where her divorce papers from my father were and she had to have proof of custody in order to sign for me.

While we waited for all of that digging to go on, we got our blood tests. And, Eureka! After a couple of hours, they found the paperwork, and we got our marriage license.

While we were downtown, getting all of that taken care of, Scotty was on the phone with everyone he knew from a baker to an Episcopal priest. When we walked in, I heard him say, "Yes! Of course, we want the people on top of the cake!" It made me laugh.

After that call, he contacted a personal friend of his who happened to be an Episcopal priest. Since Dave was baptized and confirmed in the Episcopal church, this made sense to me. I hadn't given any thought to whether I had to be Episcopalian or not.

Religion wasn't something I was comfortable with. All the 'hellfire and damnation.' in the Southern Baptist church had turned me off at a very early age. Not to mention the crazy 'holy roller' church Al's step-mother dragged me to!

I don't remember how I ended up alone with this woman, Hazel, but I'll never forget it. I was maybe eight years old, and for some reason, I was left at her house one afternoon. Al and his father had gone hunting or fishing, and Hazel was my babysitter. I barely knew her. We didn't visit his father often. They lived out in the boondocks in a shack surrounded by sand and scrub brush.

Hazel was an alcoholic. She would put a bottle of beer under her bed at night so she could drink it before she got out of bed in the morning. I don't recall seeing her without a beer in her hand or nearby.

I kept myself in front of the TV most of the afternoon, and around dusk, Hazel went upstairs. I thought she might be going to bed since she'd had quite a few beers already.

A little while later she came down the stairs in a dress and donning a big flowery hat. I was very surprised to see her like that and more surprised when she said, "Get in the car, kid, we're going to church."

She never struck me as a church-goer, and it wasn't a holiday, at least that I knew of. I had no choice but to go with her. We drove further out into the country and turned onto a dirt road. At the end of the road was a small wood framed building with a steeple.

There were a few more cars there but not a lot. The place couldn't have held more than a dozen or two. We sat in the back pew. A few minutes went by and a woman in a billowy flowery smock, wearing a conical headpiece, came down the aisle. A guy started playing the organ, and things began to stir. The woman reached the lectern and began to speak. At first, I understood her but, suddenly she started speaking gobblety gook. It didn't sound like another language, just nonsense. She was speaking in tongues.

Whatever she was saying turned the whole place into a circus. People were doing flips down the aisle, dancing around speaking nonsense, it was scary! Hazel didn't join in; exactly, she stayed next to me. But, after a short time, she began to speak nonsense, too and, I hid under the pew.

I have no idea how long this went on but, it seemed an eternity. Then the noise abated as people exited the building and Hazel reached a hand to me. I took her hand, and we left. She didn't say a word the whole way back.

Daddy duJour

When we reached her house, I was very relieved to see Al's car there. He asked where we'd been and I shrugged because I simply couldn't explain it. Hazel told him we'd gone to church.

"Oh for crying out loud," Al's dad said, "you took the poor kid to that crazy place?"

Hazel flipped him the bird and went upstairs.

When Scotty got off the phone, he told us we needed to go to the church at 2pm and go through some paperwork beforehand. The wedding would be at 5:30pm. That gave me some time in between to pull myself together, in every sense.

First order of business was getting witnesses for the marriage. I couldn't reach Nadine, who was my first choice as Maid of Honor, but I did call a high school friend, and she agreed. She had recently had a baby and she had to borrow clothes to wear but, she showed up, and I was grateful.

Dave contacted his college roommate, and miraculously he was available. It was all happening at once!

Dave's parents arrived shortly before our meeting with the priest, and all six of us went to the church. I guess it was because there might be signatures needed but, honestly, I don't remember.

The family waited outside of the minister's office while we answered questions inside. I can't recall most of the things he asked but, everything came to a halt when he asked Dave if he had been baptized and confirmed and Dave replied, "Yes."

Then, of course, he asked me the same thing. I said, "No."

"You haven't been confirmed?" he asked.

"I haven't been baptized or confirmed," I answered.

stunned silence

"Would you like to be baptized?" he asked.

Now, in the Baptist religion, which was the one I was familiar with, thanks to my grandparents, baptism was being dunked in a large tank of water, resembling an oversized fish tank. Some people were dunked in a lake or some other body of water but, most of the Baptist churches I'd ever been in it was a huge tank behind the altar.

I was aware, however, that the Episcopalians were more conservative with the amount of water used and simply splashed your forehead. So, after considerable thought, I looked at Dave who shrugged his shoulders, and I said, "Sure, why not?" We walked out of the minister's office, and my mother asked, "What's happening now?"

"He's going to baptize me," I said.

We all just sort of stared at each other and almost laughed. This day was becoming more memorable by the moment.

Daddy duJour

To make it even more unforgettable, I needed two witnesses for the baptism, and that's when Scotty and Dave became my Godparent's. Perfect, really.

After the baptism we had a few hours before the wedding ceremony so, mom and I decided to go shopping for a wedding dress. I did have the two choices I brought with me but, when she offered to buy, I thought, why not.

We never found anything I liked as well as the dresses I'd brought, so we gave up. When we got back to the house, Dave was in his suit pacing the floor. Our friends were due to stop by anytime, and I had to get myself together quickly.

I remember sitting in the bathtub rerunning the past two days in my head and feeling a bit numb. Everything happened so quickly there hadn't been time to think about the big picture.

What would it be like living in New York? The mere thought gave me butterflies in my stomach but, in a good way. I loved seeing Boston and the ocean. We would be close to the ocean and New York City.

Everything ahead of me was unknown except for the man I would be with. That made me smile. There had been more unexpected surprises in my life than many eighteen-year-olds have experienced, and most of them were not good. I knew October 2, 1968, was a turning point that would be life-altering in the best possible way.

I finished getting dressed and walked out to the living room to see Dave pacing. He looked at me and smiled. We were ready!

Everyone arrived, and we were off to the church.

Somehow this crazy rushed wedding became a very intimate and loving ceremony in a beautiful church. We have Scotty to thank for that. When I think of what we might have had, had we gone to some Justice of the Peace, in Indiana, it makes me shudder.

Dave's dad brought his Kodak camera and ran out of film. The church secretary gave him a roll of black and white film. Someone had a Polaroid camera, and the finished wedding album was completely representative of this amazing melange we patched together.

Back at the house, there was a beautiful wedding cake, with the people on the top, sitting on the table and several bottles of champagne. I think someone brought a tray of sandwiches from a deli. I'm not sure. My head was still in the clouds as this amazing day wound down.

A light rain was falling when we left the church. It had become a deluge by the time we had changed our clothes and packed up the car to head out. If it hadn't been raining we might have driven back to Butler but, it didn't seem worth the stress, so we stopped at a Holiday Inn by the turnpike.

Funny aside: Dave's parents told us they, too, had stopped at a motel by the turnpike but, they drove around the parking lot first to make sure we weren't there. They thought it might be awkward running into us the next morning. That still makes me chuckle whenever I think about it.

Daddy duJour

Dave had sold his Spitfire and bought his dad's old VW Bug a month or so before the wedding. When we got back to Butler, we packed up my apartment and all of Dave's things he had left at his parents and squeezed them into the Bug. Talk about humble beginnings!

Kmart had given Dave a couple of extra days off for the move, so we turned the drive from Pittsburgh to Scarsdale into a honeymoon through Amish Country. Pennsylvania is a beautiful state, and we thoroughly enjoyed a brief time to relax and enjoy it. October is my favorite month of the year.

Epilogue

October 2, 2018, Dave and I celebrated our 50th anniversary. I can't believe it. Well, that's not exactly true. If you can learn from others mistakes, it can help you avoid them yourself. I feel that's what has kept us together all these years.

When I tell people, we've been married 50 years. I follow that with, "10 years of wedded bliss, not necessarily consecutive". We laugh about it but, it's true.

I watched my mother's relationships go from madly in love to good riddance. Not just the ones she married, either. She was never without a man in her life somehow. Everything she embodied I swore I would never be.

Both of my parents are narcissists. I believe it's a trait you inherit and I'm forever grateful I did not. Mom is also bi-polar.

I would like to share one more story.

Dave and I have two sons. They are twenty months apart. After the beating from Les and being told I might not be able to have children, I wasn't careful with birth control. So, instant kids! We chose to have them close together. After our second son was born, I spent about four years trying to find a doctor who would tie my tubes. I felt, in some ways, I had already raised two sons, and I didn't want any more children. Period. The procedure was done when our youngest was in pre-kindergarten. Whew!

Fast forward to May 1988.

It seemed I was in constant conflict with my teenage sons. I'm usually more comfortable with teenagers than toddlers. Dave suggested I share some of my childhood experiences with them. He reasoned it would give them insight if they knew more about my upbringing and why they hadn't seen or heard from their grandmother in thirteen years.

I always hoped she would reach out to them and attempt a relationship she never had with her own children. I didn't want to slant their view of her, even though she swore I had poisoned their minds against her. Nothing could have been further from the truth.

Dave was right. It was time. Somehow Mother's Day seemed a good time to have this little chat. It made for very interesting dinner conversation, believe me.

A few days after my family History conversation I got a call from my uncle Ralph in Georgia. My grandfather was dying. He hadn't been in great health for a while, and a recent stroke was the last straw. I had to get there as soon as possible. My sons insisted on going with me.

Granddaddy and I were very close. There was the time I thought he would 'beat my ass' as my mother wanted him to but, all he did was tell me to scream as he hit the bed with his belt to appease my mother. I've never forgotten that.

Barbara Hammond

We were living in Pittsburgh, PA at the time and I had just gotten a new BMW 325 Convertible. I felt confident about driving straight through to Georgia in one day, even though neither of the boys had their drivers license and couldn't share the load.

As we drove into West Virginia every light on the dashboard lit up like a Christmas tree! There was no power, and I was mesmerized by the dash flashing. Thankfully my son grabbed the wheel and pulled us into a rest area!

We were less than two hours from home so I called Dave thinking he could come to save us. He said, "Check the owner's manual for BMW dealers in West Virginia. There has to be one."

It turned out there were three and one was on our route about ninety miles away. I contacted them, and they recommended a towing service and told me to make sure they brought a flatbed truck.

I have to tell you, even though my entire family is from rural Georgia and some are total hicks, I was unprepared for the tow truck driver. He was straight out of the movie, Deliverance! Dirty, smelly, sporting 'summer teeth.' You know, some are here...some are there?

He told the boys they could ride in the car on top of the flatbed. I would ride in the cab of the truck with him. My sons protested, but I told them it would be fine. Our chauffeur was disgusting, but he didn't seem threatening.

Daddy duJour

Once we got on the road, I kept thinking, "I can do this! We'll be fine. It's only ninety miles." It took three hours.

There wasn't much conversation in the truck. I asked him if I could smoke, (It was 1988). He had no problem with that. After I lit up, I began looking for an ashtray. There wasn't one. When I asked him about it, he said, "Aww shoot, you can use my spit cup." I immediately threw the cigarette out the window. I did not want to hear the sss when it hit!

We made it to the dealership, and they spent an hour analyzing the car. It would need a special part from Germany and take a day or two. So much for making it in one day. We arranged for a rental car and went to get a bite to eat.

Having grown up primarily on the Northeast Coast, the boys were unfamiliar with Southern hospitality and accents. The waitress who called us all 'Hun' had asked my seventeen year old if he'd like 'Franch' or Ranch on his salad and when she walked away he said, "I feel like I have YANKEE tattooed on my forehead." We all laughed.

At that point, I realized how special this trip really was. In spite of the car fiasco, we were enjoying each other more than we had in a long time. We were bonding as adults, which they had become right before my eyes.

We spent the night in Knoxville, TN and rode into Georgia early the next morning. I remember my guilt about speeding. What a bad example I was setting! But, I didn't want to arrive too late.

Barbara Hammond

At one point I must have been doing 90mph, and a driver up ahead put his hand out the window and signaled me to slow down. I thought, AHA, he has a radar detector!

Sure enough, we passed a speed trap, and he put his arm out urging me to carry on. The boys thought that was so cool. Ok, not the best motherly example, I'll admit.

We made good time and went straight to the hospital when we got to Rome, GA. As we moved off the elevator, I looked down the hallway and saw a woman step out at the other end.

I said, "There's, your grandmother." "No way," was their response.

I couldn't even recall the last time I'd seen her. She was a bit rounder than I remembered. She was now fifty-five years old, still trying to rock the mini-skirt. The make-up reminded me of the movie, "Whatever Happened to Baby Jane."

She ran toward us as soon as she realized who it was. Gushing would be an understatement.

"Ohhh, my babies!! I've missed you so much!!" were her first words to the grandsons she'd had no contact with for thirteen years.

She was cordial to me. It always started out that way then without warning it would get ugly. At that moment I was more interested in seeing Granddaddy.

Daddy duJour

He was awake, alert and waiting for us. I hoped my face didn't reveal the horror I felt looking at this skeleton that used to be my big strong grandfather.

My brother, David, was there. The one I ran away with all those years ago. I hadn't seen him in a while, and it was good to have him there. He's a gentle soul.

My aunt was there, as were my two uncles. Curiously, my grandmother wasn't anywhere to be seen. When I asked about her, my mother went into a tirade, as if Granddaddy couldn't hear her.

"If that was mother laying there daddy wouldn't leave her side!" she said. "She's been here once in two days, and I know he's wondering where she is."

"Has anyone asked her why?" David asked.

Of course, no one had asked her anything.

After spending some time with Granddaddy my brother and I went out to visit my grandmother. The boys went to my aunt's house. She was preparing a big dinner for everyone.

Mamaw, as we lovingly called her, was in the house with the drapes drawn and no lights on. It was mid-day but very dark and foreboding in her house. The quiet was deafening.

She could talk anyone's ear off anytime day or night. She didn't have conversations as much as monologues. It was an endearing quality once you got to know her. This day she was very quiet.

We coaxed her out onto the porch for some fresh air and to chat a bit. As we sat there catching up, since we hadn't seen her in quite a while, my brother told her what some were saying about her absence and asked her how she was holding up.

She didn't respond right away. She was staring out at the garden that was Granddaddy's pride and joy. I could tell she was trying not to cry. I could count on one hand the times I'd ever seen her cry.

She composed herself and looked at us directly. "I've loved that man my whole life. I just can't watch him die."

As far as we were concerned, that was all the explanation needed. We had experienced the love they had for each other all of our lives. I've never known two people more devoted. We knew Granddaddy understood completely.

My aunt had invited Mamaw to dinner, and we convinced her to come with us. It was a full house with aunts, uncles, and cousins. As we reached the end of the meal and some were meandering out onto the porch, my mother started accusing Mamaw of not loving Granddaddy enough.

I ran interference, and in no time at all, she redirected her venom at me. It was always the same. She lives in the past and in her past everyone was out to ruin her life. Six failed marriages and none were her fault. A few of them, apparently, was my fault. She is a very sad creature.

Daddy duJour

By the time the kids and I were ready to head back North the next morning my grandfather had been moved to hospice care. We stopped to see him before we left. My mother and aunt were sitting in his room.

Granddaddy was glad to see us, as always. He motioned for my son to come closer and closer, then he reached up and grabbed his Red Sox hat off his head and flipped it inside out. Granddaddy was a Detroit Tiger fan. The big grin on his face was the perfect memory for us!

We all hugged my aunt and said our goodbyes as my mother sat there staring off in the other direction. My aunt said, "Aren't you going to say goodbye to Barb and the boys?"

She stiffened up and waved us off.

That's the last time we ever saw her.

About the Author

Barbara Hammond is an artist, children's book author of The Duffy Chronicles, and blogger at Zero to 60 and beyond. She's been married to her husband, Dave, for over 50 years and, has two grown sons and three grandsons.

Barbara and her family have moved many times over the years, due to Dave's career in retail. With each move, Barbara found ways to re-invent herself. She worked in the fashion modeling profession at an agency in Philadelphia and, after several years and a move to Massachusetts, she opened her own modeling agency.

She and Dave owned a health spa for a few years, in Massachusetts, and then came another transfer and a move to Pittsburgh, PA. Barbara dabbled in Real Estate there but, didn't really enjoy it. Then she found a job that she and Dave both enjoyed, radio sales.

Working in sales at a classic rock radio station was fun. The owners of the station became close friends, and they all attended the concerts together.

After a few years, they were back in Philadelphia. Barbara went back to the modeling agency to begin a talent division. It involved working with actors from NYC and Philadelphia and, she enjoyed it very much.

Today, Barbara and Dave are retired and, living at the Jersey Shore.

"Actually, Dave is retired, and I'm writing and creating art, which is sometimes like a job," Barbara says.

Made in the USA
Middletown, DE
22 April 2019